Contents

Welcome to the Journey

When you decided to explore ESSENTIAL BIBLE PASSAGES, you accepted an invitation to take an exciting journey. Some of you may be taking this journey on your own (without being involved in a class or a group). If so, this student book can be used as a guide to help you do that. Most of you will be taking the journey with others, and this book will also be your guide along with additional direction you will receive from your leader.

If you are using this book in a group setting, you may find that diversity within the group will make your exploration even more interesting:

➤ Some of you may have never explored the Bible before, so every trail is brand-new territory.

➤ Others in the group have already been reading the Bible for a while, so several trails will have familiar landmarks.

➤ Many of you will probably find yourselves somewhere in between these two stages of familiarity with the Bible.

➤ *All of you will have something to contribute to the adventure.* Each participant may see or hear something that the others may not have noticed. And isn't that possibility of

discovering "something new" at the heart of any adventure?

Whether on your own or in a group, there are two ways to make the journey. (1) One is to *start at the beginning and travel to the end.* If you do that, you will find that the sessions have been planned to help you move through the Bible and to get an idea of its flow and its relationships. (2) The other way is to take *eighteen short trips* according to your interest. You or the group might want to study the Twenty-third Psalm one week and then the Lord's Prayer the next.

As with any journey there are a variety of different experiences that await you. Some passages will seem to offer a magnificent view as if from a mountaintop. Other passages will seem like some half-hidden object in the middle of the path. Once you start to dig it up, however, you find that a priceless treasure lies beneath the surface.

Finally, our hope and our prayer are that you will discover that ESSENTIAL BIBLE PASSAGES will be an important part of your lifelong adventure with the Bible.

–Branson L. Thurston, Editor

ESSENTIAL BIBLE PASSAGES FOR YOUTH

And God Said, "Let There Be. ..." and It Was Good

God saw everything that [God] had made, and indeed, it was very good.

(Genesis 1:31)

Searching For...

> ➤ what Genesis 1:1–2:4 tells me about the Creation
> ➤ what I can learn about God from this story
> ➤ what the Creation story helps me to know about how God works in my life
> ➤ I also want to know...

Setting Out on the Journey

1. Read Genesis 1:1–2:4.
2. Fold a sheet of paper into eight sections. Write in the first block on the left, "The Story of Creation According to Genesis 1:1–2:4." At the bottom of each of the other seven blocks, write one of these references:
   > ➤ Day 1—Genesis 1:1-5;
   > ➤ Day 2—Genesis 1:6-8;
   > ➤ Day 3—Genesis 1:9-13;
   > ➤ Day 4—Genesis 1:14-19;
   > ➤ Day 5—Genesis 1:20-23;
   > ➤ Day 6—Genesis 1:24-31;
   > ➤ Day 7—Genesis 2:1-4.
3. After you have read about each day of the Creation, draw what happened as you imagine it, in each block of your sheet of paper.

Getting Your Bearings

Review Genesis 1:1–2:4 to see how it points you in these directions:

➤ God created order out of chaos.
➤ God saw that all of creation was good.
➤ God created humanity in God's own image.
➤ God rested and gave the gift of sabbath rest to humans as well.

Exploring the Past

Many societies tell stories of creation because people want to know how the universe started. Where did the Milky Way, the Rock of Gibraltar, the Pacific Ocean, and mallard ducks begin? Where did humans come from and, perhaps most importantly, why are we here?

The Hebrew people actually have two accounts to address these big questions. Both were handed down from generation to generation before being written in their present form. The older one, found in Genesis 2:5-25, was probably written down during King Solomon's reign (961–928 B.C.), though it was likely told long before then around camp-fires. In that story, God is an intimate friend who created humanity out of mud and walked with Adam and Eve in the garden of Eden.

On the other hand, Genesis 1 portrays God as a powerful sovereign whose very word creates and brings order out of chaos. When the account in Genesis 1 was written down, most of the population of Jerusalem was living in chaos as exiles in Babylon. King Nebuchadnezzar had first attacked Jerusalem in 597 B.C. and finally burned it down in 587 B.C. Despite this defeat, the exiles never doubted that God was in charge. They believed that God used the Babylonians to punish them for their continuing worship of idols and unfair treatment of others. Genesis 1 helped to reflect the captives' hope that God would create order in their out-of-control world. God did just that. In 538 B.C., King Cyrus of Persia issued a decree allowing the Israelites to return home and rebuild.

Pulling Together

Order out of Chaos

As the youth group from Centerville surveyed the flood damage they had come to help repair in Marlow, Jeffrey exclaimed, "Nobody will ever be able to fix this mess." Most of the other group members nodded their heads in agreement. Then Rita pointed out that they had come too far just to give up before they got started. So for five days they piled debris into pick-up trucks, swept sand out of houses, and tried their best to clean what was left. When it was time to return home, one of the residents thanked the group for working on her house. She also remarked that the youth had brought some order out of the chaos and some hope that her life could be rebuilt.

➤ How do you see God's creative work being carried out in this scene?

➤ What examples can you think of in which your youth group can work together to bring order to a chaotic situation?

God Told Humans to Care For Creation

God saw that all of creation was good. After God created humanity, God entrusted the Earth and its creatures to people with the expectation that humans would be good stewards and caretakers.

➤ What do you think God might be saying about the way people are treating creation today? Give specific examples of actions that you think cause God pain and others that make God happy.

➤ What specific action can you and your group take to show responsible care for the Earth and the creatures and people who live on it?

God Gives the Gift of Sabbath Rest

God rested on the seventh day, called the sabbath. In Jewish tradition, the sabbath begins at sundown on Friday and ends at sundown on Saturday. Most Christians call Sunday the sabbath, though it was originally known as the Lord's Day because this is the day on which Jesus was resurrected from the dead. The important point is that people of both faiths—Christianity and Judaism—observe a day of rest.

➤ Why is a day of sabbath rest important to people's minds and souls and bodies?

➤ What agreement can you make with the other members of your group about taking a sabbath? How can you, together, influence the scheduling of community activities, such as sports, so as to have a day of sabbath rest?

All Things Bright and Beautiful

All things bright and beau - ti - ful, all crea-tures great and _ small,

Fine

all things wise and won - der - ful; the Lord God made them _ all.

1. Each lit - tle flower that _ o - pens, each lit - tle bird _ that sings, God _
2. The pur - ple head - ed _ moun-tains, the ri - ver run - ning by, the _
3. The cold wind in the _ win - ter, the pleas-ant sum - mer sun, the _
4. God gave us eyes to _ see them, and lips _ that we _ might tell how _

made their glow-ing _ col - ors, and _ made their ti - ny ___ wings.
sun - set and the _ morn - ing that _ bright-ens up the ___ sky.
ripe fruits in the _ gar - den: God _ made them ev - ery ___ one.
great is God Al - might - y, who _ has made all things _ well.

WORDS: Cecil Frances Alexander, 1848 (Gen. 1: 31)
MUSIC: 17th. cent. English melody; arr. by Martin Shaw, 1915

God's creative power brings order out of chaos. What "chaos" are you experiencing in your own life, or in your family, right now? Are you having trouble with your parents, brothers or sisters, friends, school, or work? What problems do you need to solve with God's help? What difference does it make to you to know that God has created—and is in charge of—an orderly cosmos?

Is your own life so hectic that you are missing out on the gift of God's sabbath rest? If so, what changes can you make in your schedule that will allow you to enter into a time of rest and re-creation?

If people tried to describe what God was like by observing you, what would they say? Of course, "God is spirit" (John 4:24), not a person of a particular gender or age or ethnic group or nationality. But each person is created to have fellowship with God, to have God's Holy Spirit living in him or her. Therefore, you bear God's spiritual image. How would your actions and words be different if you took seriously the idea that you are created in the image of God?

What are you currently doing to care for God's creation? What could you be doing to be a better steward (or caretaker) of the people, plants, animals, air, water, and rocks of God's good earth?

The World as the Early Readers of Genesis 1:1–2:4 Saw It

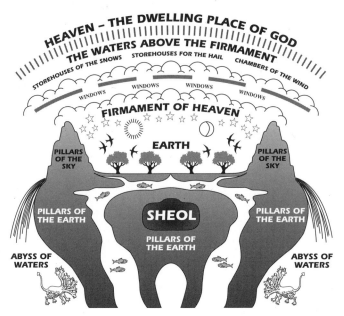

Praise to God for Creation
Psalm 104:1-6

(A) Bless the LORD, O my soul.

(B) O LORD my God, you are very great.

(C) You are clothed with honor and majesty,
wrapped in light as with a garment.

(D) You stretch out the heavens like a tent,
you set the beams of your chambers on the waters,

(E) you make the clouds your chariot,
you ride on the wings of the wind,

(F) you make the winds your messengers,
fire and flame your ministers.

(G) You set the earth on its foundations,
so that it shall never be shaken.

(H) You cover it with the deep as with a garment;
the waters stood above the mountains.

"Moses, Moses!"

When the LORD saw
that he had turned aside to see,
God called to him out of the bush,
"Moses, Moses!"
And he said, "Here I am."

(Exodus 3:4)

Searching For...

> ➤ what the story in Exodus tells me about God's calling of ordinary people, including me, to accomplish God's purposes;
> ➤ an understanding of how Moses responded to God's call;
> ➤ the meaning of the divine name;
> ➤ I also want to know . . .

Setting Out on the Journey

1. Read Exodus 3:1-15.
2. Put yourself in Moses' place. You're out doing your regular work when God calls you. How would you have felt? What would you have asked God? What would your answer to God's call have been?

3. Now put yourself in God's place. Why did you get involved in human affairs? Why did you choose a human being for the job when you have the power to perform a miracle to free the Israelites?

Getting Your Bearings

Look again at Exodus 3:1-15 to see how it points you in these directions:

➤ God is so deeply concerned about humanity that God gets involved in human history.
➤ God acts on behalf of those who suffer.
➤ God uses ordinary people who think they have no special skills or status to do God's work in the world.
➤ God's name is I AM WHO I AM.

Exploring the Past

The Hebrew people had come from Israel to Egypt during a famine that occurred about four hundred years before Moses' birth. A young Hebrew named Joseph, who was sold into slavery by his jealous brothers, had been put in charge of the Egyptian food supply. Joseph gained this assignment because he correctly interpreted the pharaoh's dream about the serious famine that was to come. To avoid starvation, Joseph's family came to Egypt seeking food. They decided to stay. Although the Hebrews had come to Egypt voluntarily, they ended up as slaves.

Just before Moses' birth, the Egyptian pharaoh (probably Seti I) began to fear that the growing Hebrew population would side with his enemies in the case of an attack. The pharaoh ordered all male babies killed. Moses' mother hid him for a few months and then made a waterproof basket for him. She set Moses in the basket near the river's edge where he was rescued by the pharaoh's daughter, who raised him as her own child.

As an adult, Moses fled Egypt after he killed an Egyptian taskmaster who was beating a Hebrew slave. Moses settled in Midian, where he married Zipporah, the daughter of a Midianite priest. Moses was tending the sheep flock of his father-in-law, Jethro, when God spoke to him out of the burning bush. God called Moses to deliver the Hebrews from their slavery in Egypt. Moses stalled for a while, asking God many questions; finally, he agreed to serve God.

Pulling Together

God's Call

"God is calling me? You've got to be kidding," Sean laughed. "Moses was one more awesome dude. I am definitely not in that guy's league, or even in that ballpark. No way am I going up against the Rattlers. They are totally tough."

"Laugh if you want to. But I believe that God wants to use you and all of us to make a witness about the gang fights that have been going on in our neighborhood. I think we should begin by being nice to some of the gang members at school, including the ones who belong to the Rattlers. We need to reach out with the love of Jesus and let these kids know that people want to respect them and to be friendly. I know we can do this," concluded Nikki as she ended her speech to the youth group.

➤ What might God be calling your youth group to do? Are there some big tasks that ordinary people like you can do in your school or community? Think especially of situations where determination and courage are needed to stand against an individual or a group that causes suffering for others.

Support for the Journey

After Moses answered God's call, God gave him resources for his spiritual and physical journey with the Hebrew people. Later in Exodus you will learn that God asked Moses' brother Aaron and his sister Miriam to help Moses. God led the Hebrews with a pillar of cloud and a pillar of fire. God also sent manna (bread) from heaven to feed the people as they wandered in the desert. Most of all, God said to Moses, "I will be with you" (Exodus 3:12a); and God was indeed present all the time.

➤ How do you experience God's presence with you?

➤ Think of a particular task you have to do. What resources does God give you to do this task?

➤ How is the community of faith—perhaps your youth group or the whole church—a resource for your journey of faith? How do others help and support you? What can you do together that you could not do alone?

Highlights of Moses' Journey of Faith

Moses is born, hidden, and saved from death.
(Exodus 2:1-10)

Moses kills an Egyptian taskmaster.
(Exodus 2:11-15a)

Moses escapes to Midian, marries, and has a son.
(Exodus 2:15b-22)

The Hebrew slaves in Egypt cry to God for salvation.
(Exodus 2:23-25)

God calls Moses for service.
(Exodus 3:1–4:17)

Moses and his family leave for Egypt.
(Exodus 4:18-20)

At God's command, Moses goes to Pharaoh to tell him to let God's people go; but Pharaoh repeatedly says no.
(Exodus 5:1–11:10)

Moses gives God's directions for the Passover and leads the people out of Egypt, across the Red Sea.
(Exodus 12:1–14:31)

Moses leads the Israelites in celebrating their escape, and they go into the wilderness.
(Exodus 15:1–19:25)

God gives Moses the Ten Commandments.
(Exodus 20:1-17 and Deuteronomy 5:1-21)

Moses leads the Hebrew people in the wilderness for forty years.
(summary in Deuteronomy 1:1–3:29)

Moses dies at age 120, but no one knows exactly where he is buried.
(Deuteronomy 34:1-12)

God continues to call people today. Perhaps God is calling you right now, or has called you in the past. Think about a time when God seemed to be calling you to do something. Maybe God spoke to you through someone who needed help. Where were you? What were you doing? What made you think God was speaking to you even if there was no burning bush to get your attention? What was your response? Write some words or phrases in the space below to remind you of this incident.

The story in Exodus shows that God does act in response to human suffering. In the space below write a conversation between yourself and God in which you tell God about a problem you have and the kind of help you need. Be sure to include what you think God would say in response.

I really need to talk with you, God. I want to tell you about this problem I have. It all started when . . .

God told Moses the divine name, I AM WHO I AM. The Bible uses many names to refer to God, such as Lord, Shepherd, Creator, Father, and Yahweh. Which of God's possible names appeal to you? List a few of your favorites in the space below. If there is a reason these names are especially meaningful to you, write the reason beside the name.

Go Down, Moses

[African American spiritual based on Exodus 3:7-12]

1. When Israel was in Egypt's land, let my people go;
   oppressed so hard they could not stand, let my people go.

Refrain (after each verse)
Go down, (go down) Moses, (Moses) way down in Egypt's land;
tell old Pharaoh to let my people go!

2. "Thus saith the Lord," bold Moses said, let my people go;
   "if not, I'll smite your firstborn dead," let my people go.

3. No more shall they in bondage toil, let my people go;
   let them come out with Egypt's spoil, let my people go.

4. We need not always weep and mourn, let my people go;
   and wear those slavery chains forlorn, let my people go.

5. Come, Moses, you will not get lost, let my people go;
   stretch out your rod and come across, let my people go.

****

May the presence of God the Creator give you strength;
May the presence of God the Redeemer give you peace;
May the presence of God the Sustainer give you comfort;
May the presence of God the Sanctifier give you love. Amen.[1]

[1] From *1987 United Methodist Clergywomen's Consultation Resource Book*; page 67.
Quoted in *The United Methodist Book of Worship* (Copyright © 1992 The United Methodist
Publishing House); page 563. Used by permission.

The Passover

Your children will ask you, "What are we celebrating?" And you will answer, "The Passover animal is killed to honor the LORD. We do these things because on that night long ago the LORD passed over the homes of our people in Egypt."

(Exodus 12:26-27a, *The Contemporary English Version*)

Searching For...

➤ what the Passover and the Exodus were about;
➤ an understanding of the difference that the Passover and the Exodus made in the lives of the Hebrew people who experienced them;
➤ how I can experience God's saving and liberating presence in my own life;
➤ I also want to know . . .

Setting Out on the Journey

1. Read Exodus 12:21-32.
2. Try to put yourself in the place of the following people: Moses, one of the Hebrew slaves in Egypt, and Pharaoh. In each case, how would you have reacted to the events described in this passage?

3. How would you retell this story so that a child could understand it?

Getting Your Bearings

Review Exodus 12:21-32 to see how it points you in these directions:

➤ God commanded Moses to tell the Hebrew people, who were then slaves in Egypt, to sacrifice a lamb in each household and smear its blood over the doorway of the house.
➤ Because the Egyptian king had repeatedly refused to release the Hebrews from slavery, God planned to punish the Egyptians by killing the firstborn male in each of their households.
➤ God told Moses that the night of Passover was to be remembered from generation to generation.
➤ After the Egyptians realized that their firstborn males had died, the Hebrew people hurriedly left the country at God's direction.

Exploring the Past

Although the original Passover and the escape from Egypt occurred sometime between 1250 and 1225 B.C., Passover is to this day an extremely important Jewish festival. Jewish families gather together to eat foods that remind them of their hasty departure from Egypt. The story of the Passover is told around the dinner table, just as Exodus 12:26-27a said it was to be.

At the time of the Passover, the Hebrew people were slaves in Egypt. They had come to Egypt about four hundred years before the time of the Exodus to escape a famine in Israel. Over the years, they had become slaves. In their oppressed condition they cried out to God, who answered them by raising up Moses to lead them out of Egypt and into the land that God had promised to Abraham.

At God's command, Moses had tried repeatedly to convince Pharaoh to let the people go. He repeatedly refused, even though plagues of frogs, gnats, boils, darkness, and other things followed each refusal. Finally, God intended to punish Pharaoh and his people by killing the firstborn male in each Egyptian household, while passing over the homes of the Hebrews. (Their homes were to be marked with the blood of a sacrificed lamb.) After this event occurred, the Hebrew people left Egypt and followed Moses (and God, who appeared as a pillar of cloud and a pillar of fire) into the wilderness as free people.

Pulling Together

Seeking Freedom

As you study this lesson, where throughout the world are people seeking freedom? Are there people who are under the thumb of a dictator? Where are there victims of war? Are there people who lack food because a greedy or corrupt government is blocking the shipment of supplies? Are there people, perhaps in your own city or town, whose reading skills are so poor that they cannot get a decent job? How might God act to free these people? Do you believe that God will act? What part might the Christian church play? What role might you and your classmates play?

Celebrating Passover

Passover is a time when Jewish families gather together to celebrate God's saving action in Egypt. They prepare special foods. They use traditional rituals that have been handed down for generations. Similarly, Christian families use special foods, traditions, and rituals to celebrate holy days, especially Christmas and Easter. How does your own family celebrate Christmas and/or Easter? Do you know some of the reasons certain family traditions were begun and continued? How does your church celebrate these holidays? What special traditions do you have as a congregation?

On the Journey

The people left Egypt and went into the wilderness as God directed them. Their final destination, the Promised Land, was a long way off. The journey was not easy. The people complained a lot, blaming both Moses and God for their problems. But God always provided for the Hebrews. Moreover, the people found safety in numbers. If only one or two persons had been all alone in the wilderness, they might have been killed by wild animals or might have found it impossible to survive.

Christians also speak about being on a journey of faith. God guides us individually and as a community of faith. Just as God gave the Hebrew people manna (bread) in the wilderness, pillars of fire and cloud to guide them, and a human leader named Moses, God gives Christians resources for the journey. What are some of those people, traditions, beliefs, and other resources that enable you and your classmates to journey in faith? What other resources do you think you need?

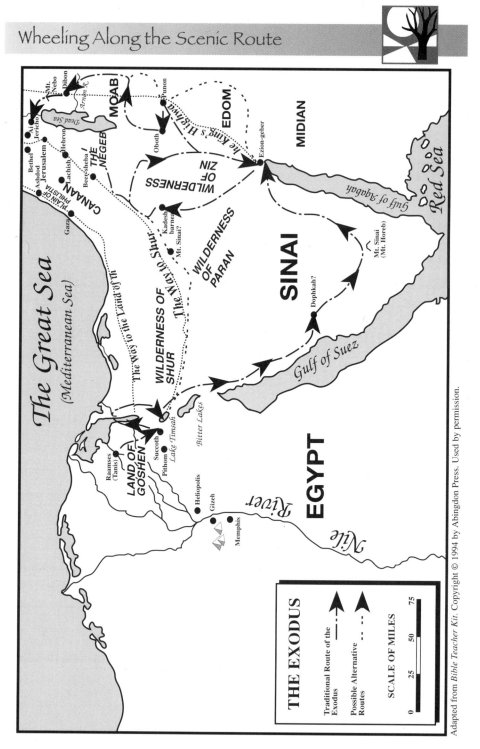

THE EXODUS

Traditional Route of the Exodus

Possible Alternative Routes

SCALE OF MILES

0   25   50   75

Adapted from *Bible Teacher Kit*. Copyright © 1994 by Abingdon Press. Used by permission.

Reflecting On the Journey

Christians understand the story of the Passover and the Exodus to be their story as well as that of the Hebrew people. In 1 Corinthians 5:7, Paul writes about Christ, our paschal (Passover) lamb, who has been sacrificed. Just as God freed the slaves from Egypt, God frees Christians from sin.

What is oppressing you? Are there sinful habits, relationships, behaviors, or attitudes that are holding you tightly in their grip? Spend some time in prayer asking God to free you from whatever is enslaving you. Invite Jesus, the Passover lamb of God, to lead you to freedom. (You may want to record your thoughts here.)

The Passover story and the flight from Egypt mark a critical point in the history of the Hebrew people. They are no longer slaves who are forced to make bricks from mud for Pharaoh's building projects. However, they are not yet settled in the Promised Land. They are beginning a difficult venture that will require many adjustments. During the journey in the wilderness, they raise many complaints about the lack of food and water. Some insist that Moses should have left them in Egypt. Yet, despite their complaints and their uncertainties about the future, God is faithfully leading the people.

In a way, the teen years are similar to the Exodus. You are no longer a child, though some days that might seem like a good idea. Neither are you yet an adult. Someone is always telling you what to do and how to do it. What guidance do you need from God to make this journey from childhood to adulthood? Who are some of the people who are helping you? Is there a "Moses" in your life? What questions or complaints do you want to raise to God about your life at the present time? What hopes do you have for the future? Jot down some ideas if you choose to do so.

After the Hebrew people had escaped from Pharaoh's army by crossing the Red Sea, Moses and Miriam—a prophetess who was the sister of Moses and Aaron—sang praises to God. Their songs, found in their entirety in Exodus 15:1-21, are believed to make up one of the oldest passages in the Bible.

Canticle of Moses and Miriam

Then Moses and the people of Israel sang this song to the Lord, saying,
"I will sing to the Lord, who has triumphed gloriously;
   the horse and its rider the Lord has thrown into the sea.
The Lord is my strength and my song,
   and has become my salvation;
this is my God whom I will praise.
   I will exalt my [ancestors'] God
   who is a mighty warrior,
   whose name is the Lord.
Pharaoh's chariots and his host the Lord cast into the sea;
   and his chosen officers are sunk in the Red Sea.
The floods cover them;
   they went down into the depths like a stone.
Your right hand, O Lord, glorious in power,
   your right hand, O Lord, shatters the enemy."

· ·

Then Miriam, the prophet, the sister of Aaron,
   took a timbrel in her hand;
   and all the women went out after her with timbrels and dancing,
   and Miriam sang to them:
"Sing to the Lord, who has triumphed gloriously;
   the horse and its rider the Lord has thrown into the sea." [1]

---

[1] From "Canticle of Moses and Miriam" (words adapted from Exodus 15) in *The United Methodist Hymnal* (© 1989 The United Methodist Publishing House); 135–136. Used by permission.

The Ten Commandments

Hear, O Israel, the statutes and ordinances
that I am addressing to you today;
you shall learn them and
observe them diligently.

(Deuteronomy 5:1b)

Searching For...

> ➤ what these commandments may have meant to the Hebrew people who first heard them;
> ➤ how these commandments affect my own life;
> ➤ what "covenant" means;
> ➤ I also want to know . . .

Setting Out on the Journey

1. Read Deuteronomy 5:1-21.
2. What do Moses' words (5:1-5) tell you about the way God gave the Ten Commandments?

3. What do God's words (5:8-15) tell you about how humans are to relate to God?

4. What do God's words (5:16-21) tell you about how humans are to act toward one another?

Getting Your Bearings

Review Deuteronomy 5:1-21 to see how it points you in these directions:

➤ The Ten Commandments are the core of God's covenant.
➤ The Ten Commandments make clear that we are to worship only God.
➤ The Ten Commandments set limits on behavior so that people can live together in peace and with respect for one another.
➤ The Ten Commandments still guide the lives of God's people today.

Exploring the Past

The Ten Commandments, also known as the Decalogue ("ten words"), are found in both Deuteronomy 5:1-21 and Exodus 20:1-17. Exodus records the event of God's giving the commandments. The version in Deuteronomy is part of a sermon by Moses in which he reminds the people of what God has told them and done for them. About forty years passed between the account in Exodus and Moses' sermon in Deuteronomy.

As Moses reminds the people in Deuteronomy 5:2, the Decalogue is part of God's covenant with them. (A "covenant" is a binding agreement that may be entered into by two or more people or groups, or that may involve God and humans.) In the Ten Commandments, God decides the terms of the covenant and sets forth conditions. The people can choose to either accept or reject them, but they cannot change the conditions. In accepting the covenant, the people agreed to do all that God had commanded (Exodus 24:3). In Deuteronomy 5:2, Moses reminds the people that God had made a covenant at Horeb (Mount Sinai) not only with their ancestors but with them as well. The covenant continues to be in effect.

The purpose of the Ten Commandments is to set limits on what people can and cannot do so that they might live as God's people together in harmony and with respect for one another. Jesus upheld the commandments and told his followers to do likewise (for example, Matthew 19:17-19). Therefore, the Decalogue applies to Christians now as much as it did to the Hebrews who first heard it from God in about 1250 B.C. The task of modern Christians is to understand what these commandments mean in today's society.

Pulling Together

The Ten Commandments for Today

JOSH: The Ten Commandments are history; they're old news. Rules like that don't make sense in our modern, high-tech society.

PAIGE: Just because they're old doesn't mean they don't have anything to say to us today. Why else would they be in the Bible?

TINA: I don't know, but I agree with Josh. Look at this one in Deuteronomy 5:8-9. Who's sitting around making idols these days, or bowing down to worship them?

JIM: Maybe all three of you are right. (*The others look at Jim as if he's a space alien.*) Maybe the commandments are both old and still important. I mean, Josh has a point. So does Tina, but maybe we're worshiping different kinds of idols today. For example, some teens dream about driving fast cars. Others are obsessed with the latest fashions. Still others consider only those occupations that offer lots of money and power. Can't such things be idols in our day?

JOSH: Yeah, I suppose you're right. I hadn't thought of it that way.

PAIGE: I see what you mean. After all, we know that people still envy what other people have and steal things that are not theirs.

TINA: Sure. And everybody on my block knows that our next-door neighbor and her boss are cheating on their spouses.

JIM: Some of the commandments do raise a lot of questions, though. How do we define murder? In the Old Testament we read about wars and about laws that allowed stoning people to death as punishment. Aren't those actions murder?

PAIGE: Probably. But people in Bible times didn't have to deal with questions such as when does life begin and when is somebody really dead. Scientific knowledge is so much more advanced now.

JOSH: True. I guess we really do have to figure out what it all means today.

JIM: The commandment to honor one's parents is a tough one. My mother's always nagging me to clean my room and do my homework. Moses' mother just put him in a basket at the river's edge. He didn't have to deal with all the nagging.

PAIGE: I think we need to take a closer look at these commandments and figure out what they mean to us as Christians.

JOSH: Paige is right. Let's dig a little deeper.

I am your God.

Do not make or worship images.

Do not use God's name wrongly.

Observe the sabbath and keep it holy.

Honor your parents.

Do not kill.

Do not commit adultery.

Do not steal.

Do not accuse anyone falsely.

Do not envy your neighbor.

How do these commandments help people live in a right relationship with both God and other people?

Reflecting On the Journey

Reread Deuteronomy 5:1-21. What questions do you have about what the Ten Commandments might mean to you as a follower of Christ? Write your questions in the space below.

Read the commandments as they are found in Exodus 20:1-17. What differences do you notice between this list and the one in Deuteronomy 5:1-21? Do the differences help you better understand the commandments? If so, how? Do the differences raise questions for you? If so, what are they? Write them in the space below.

Zoom in on at least three commandments that you feel are difficult to keep. Think about why these particular commandments are hard to obey. Offer a prayer asking God to forgive you for failing to be obedient and asking God to help you. In the space below, list three to five changes you need to make in your own life in order to be obedient to these commandments.

Do you think modern Christians need other commandments to help them cope with the fast-paced, high-tech lifestyles of today? If more commandments were to be added to help humans live in the twenty-first century as God intended, what would those commandments be? Write them in the space below. Why do you think these additions are needed?

Psalm 1

1 Blessed are those
who walk not in the counsel of the wicked,
nor stand in the way of sinners,
nor sit in the seat of scoffers,
2 but whose delight is in the law of God,
and who meditate on that law day and night.

**Blessed are those whose delight
is in the law of God.**

3 They are like a tree
planted by streams of water,
that yields its fruit in its season,
and its leaf does not wither.
In all that they do, they prosper.

**Blessed are those whose delight
is in the law of God.**

4 The wicked are not so,
but are like chaff which the wind drives away.
5 Therefore the wicked will not stand in the judgment,
nor sinners in the congregation of the righteous;
6 for God knows the way of the righteous,
but the way of the wicked will perish.

**Blessed are those whose delight
is in the law of God.** 1

1 From *Inclusive-Language Psalms* (The Pilgrim Press, 1987); page 1. Taken
from *An Inclusive-Language Lectionary (Readings for Years, A, B, and C),* copyright
1983, 1984, 1985 Division of Education and Ministry, National Council of the
Churches of Christ in the U.S.A. Used by permission.

ESSENTIAL BIBLE PASSAGES FOR YOUTH

The Lord Is My Shepherd

Surely goodness and mercy
shall follow me / all the days of my life, / and
I shall dwell in the house
of the LORD / my whole life long.

(Psalm 23:6)

Searching For...

> ➤ reasons why "shepherd" is a good description for God
> ➤ why the Twenty-third Psalm is meaningful to so many people
> ➤ how God can be a protective shepherd in my life
> ➤ I also want to know . . .

Setting Out on the Journey

1. Read Psalm 23. You may want to check several Bible versions.
2. Look at the action words (verbs) in this psalm. What do they say about how the shepherd treats you?

3. Try to rewrite this psalm in your own words, perhaps using an image such as "coach" or "parent," if that is more familiar to you than the image of "shepherd."

Getting Your Bearings

Review Psalm 23 to see how it points you in these directions:

➤ God is the good shepherd.
➤ The good shepherd tends and protects the sheep.
➤ Even in life's most frightening moments, God, the good shepherd, is with you.
➤ God's kindness and faithful love will be with you forever.

Exploring the Past

The Psalms are the song book and worship book of the people of Israel. They were sung during worship services. Although some of the directions (for example, Selah) to the choir director remain written in the Psalms, the music itself has been lost. From Psalms such as 150, we know that the Hebrew people used trumpets, lutes, harps, other stringed instruments, pipes, and cymbals to praise God. They also danced unto God.

Christians have inherited this book that shows how to praise God the Creator and give thanks for what God has done for individuals and for groups of people. Readers of the Psalms learn how to ask God's forgiveness when they have sinned. The Psalms also show how to ask for help from God when trouble comes.

Psalm 23 is probably the most well-known, the most loved, and the most-often said psalm. It is a song expressing trust that God will give what is needed in all circumstances. It offers assurance that God will be with you and protect you when enemies surround you. Even as death approaches, God will be present, which is why Psalm 23 is often read at funerals. Like the shepherd who must provide everything for the sheep, so they will not be lost and hungry, God takes care of humans. Knowing that God is near, you can have confidence that God will take care of you. God's people believe that God's goodness and lovingkindness will always be with them. Therefore, like the psalmist, they choose to live in God's house or in God's presence.

Pulling Together

Shared Memories

God is always present, guarding, guiding, and loving you. Sometimes, however, especially in the middle of a crisis, it's hard to know for sure that God is right there. After the difficulty has passed, you can look back and realize the ways God was with you. In some cases, God will snatch you out of a bad situation. In others, God will suffer along with you. But God will never leave you.

Recall one or more specific examples of times when God was the good shepherd in your life. Talk about these examples with someone else as a witness to God's goodness and lovingkindness.

Being a Shepherd to Others

Who in your church or community needs someone to give them extra love, care, and concern? Could it be the mother with a sick child who needs someone to watch another child while she spends time at the hospital? Is it a school classmate whose family lost everything in a fire? Maybe it's the grouchy neighbor who thinks that all teenagers are bad. Perhaps it's the child whose dad was killed last year.

Identify at least one person who needs "shepherding." What specific action can you, either as an individual or with your youth group, take to show this person the love and care of God the good shepherd?

Shepherds in the Church

Some churches have what are called shepherds groups. These members may visit those who are sick, call people who have not attended church recently to let them know that they are missed, invite visitors to come back, and help new members get acquainted.

Talk about forming a shepherds group that is run by teens for teens. Think about the ways you could care for other youth so that they might know that the loving God is present in their own life.

Wheeling Along the Scenic Route

As you read the Bible verses that follow, try to answer this question (although Psalm 23 was written long before Jesus' birth, he often used illustrations that included sheep and shepherds):

➤ How are God and Jesus like a shepherd?

O save your people, and bless your heritage; / be their shepherd, and carry them forever. (Psalm 28:9)

Give ear, O Shepherd of Israel, / you who lead Joseph like a flock! . . . / Stir up your might, / and come to save us! (Psalm 80:1-2)

[God] will feed his flock like a shepherd; / he will gather the lambs in his arms, / and carry them in his bosom, and gently lead the mother sheep. (Isaiah 40:11)

Hear the word of the LORD, O nations, / and declare it in the coastlands far away; / say, "[God] who scattered Israel will gather him, / and will keep him as a shepherd a flock." (Jeremiah 31:10)

For thus says the Lord GOD: I myself will search for my sheep, and will seek them out. As shepherds seek out their flocks when they are among their scattered sheep, so I will seek out my sheep. I will rescue them from all the places to which they have been scattered on a day of clouds and thick darkness. I will bring them out from the peoples and gather them from the countries, and will bring them into their own land; and I will feed them on the mountains of Israel, by the watercourses, and in all the inhabited parts of the land. I will feed them with good pasture, and the mountain heights of Israel shall be their pasture; there they shall lie down in good grazing land, and they shall feed on rich pasture on the mountains of Israel. I myself will be the shepherd of my sheep, and I will make them lie down, says the Lord GOD. I will seek the lost, and I will bring back the strayed, and I will bind up the injured, and I will strengthen the weak, but the fat and the strong I will destroy. I will feed them with justice. (Ezekiel 34:11-16)

As [Jesus] went ashore, he saw a great crowd; and he had compassion for them, because they were like sheep without a shepherd; and he began to teach them many things. (Mark 6:34)

[Jesus said,] I am the good shepherd. I know my own and my own know me, just as the Father knows me and I know the Father. And I lay down my life for the sheep.

(John 10:14-15)

Reflecting On the Journey

Reread Psalm 23. If you have written this psalm in your own words, read that version again too. Think about this question: Do you, like the psalmist, feel confident that God is always with you and will provide for you, no matter what? Then, in the space below, write several words or phrases that describe how your own confidence in God's continuing presence makes you feel. Or write about any doubts you have that God is always present.

Perhaps you are like a shepherd to a family pet. Or maybe you have a lot of responsibility for younger brothers and sisters, or for another child you regularly watch. Possibly you give care to an older person who needs assistance. In the space below, list some ways in which you act like a shepherd. Then think about this sentence: If I am willing to care for a person or a pet that I love, how much more is God willing to care for me.

Ask family members and friends if they can recite Psalm 23 from memory. You may be surprised by how many people can do that. Try to memorize the psalm yourself. Choose a translation of the Bible you feel comfortable with. Or select a song version such as 136 in *The United Methodist Hymnal* or the Ralph Carmichael version that follows, "The New 23rd," which also has music to accompany the words.

Keep singing or repeating one line until you have it committed to memory. (You may want to ask someone else to help you.) Then, when you are confronted with a difficult situation—an argument, a nasty customer, an unannounced quiz, a canceled date—try reciting Psalm 23 and feel God's comforting presence.

The New 23rd

Because the Lord is my Shepherd,
I have everything that I need.
He lets me rest in meadows green
and leads me beside the quiet stream.
He keeps on giving life to me
and helps me to do what honors Him the most.
Even when walking through the dark valley of death,
valley of death, I will never be afraid for He is close beside me;
Guarding, guiding all the way
He spreads a feast before me
In the presence of my enemies
He welcomes me as His special guest.
With blessing overflowing,
His goodness and unfailing kindness
shall be with me all of my life
And afterwards I will live with Him forever,
forever in His home.
Forever in His home. [1]

Here Am I. Send Me!

Then I heard the voice of the Lord saying,
"Whom shall I send, and who will go for us?"
And I said, "Here am I; send me!"

(Isaiah 6:8)

Searching For...

➤ how Isaiah was called to be a prophet
➤ Isaiah's response to his encounter with God in the Temple
➤ a sense of God's call in my own life and my response to that call
➤ I also want to know . . .

Setting Out on the Journey

1. Read Isaiah 6:1-8.
2. Close your eyes and try to imagine what Isaiah experienced in the Temple: the sight of angels attending God on a throne; the smell of smoke; the feel of a burning coal touching his lip; the sound of God's voice.
3. Had you been Isaiah, how would you have described this extraordinary experience? How would you have responded?

Getting Your Bearings

Review Isaiah 6:1-8 to see how it points you in these directions:

➤ Isaiah was called by God to be a prophet in 742 B.C., the year that King Uzziah died.
➤ Isaiah was in the Temple when he experienced the presence of God in an amazing way.
➤ Isaiah was afraid he would die because he was a sinner standing in the presence of God. The hot coal was a sign that his sin was forgiven.
➤ When Isaiah heard God ask for someone to go out on God's behalf, Isaiah said, "Here am I; send me!"

Exploring the Past

The Book of Isaiah has many beautiful and exciting passages in it. But it can also be difficult to understand because it was probably written by two (possibly three) prophets, who wrote in different time periods. Many believe that Chapters 40–55 were written by someone scholars call Second Isaiah. He began writing about 539 B.C. He had words of comfort for the Israelite exiles in Babylon and hope for their return home. In addition, some scholars believe that Chapters 56–66 were probably written between 530 and 510 B.C. A prophet referred to as Third Isaiah seems to speak in these chapters about what life is like in the restored nation.

First Isaiah, also known as Isaiah of Jerusalem, is the prophet whose call is found in Isaiah 6:1-8. He is thought to have written Chapters 1–39. He wrote words of warning to the Southern Kingdom (Judah) during the time leading up to, and following, the fall of the Northern Kingdom (Israel) to the Assyrians in 722 B.C. He speaks out against all the injustices he sees, for he knows that such circumstances displease God.

Although Isaiah 1:1 says the writer is the son of Amoz, little else is known about him. Because his call to be a prophet came in the Temple of Jerusalem, some people believe he may have been a priest. First Isaiah prophesied between 742 and 701 B.C., possibly continuing to work until 687 B.C. Amos, Hosea, and Micah were prophets at about the same time as First Isaiah.

Pulling Together

Preparing to Hear God's Call

Isaiah was in the Temple of Jerusalem, probably worshiping or serving as a priest, when he saw God. Although God can speak to us anywhere, God's house is often the place where people hear and accept God's call on their life. Sometimes the atmosphere of the sanctuary or the act of worship itself brings people closer to God.

What stirs you the most during the worship service? Which items in the sanctuary remind you that you are in the presence of God in a special place? Compare your responses with those of other members of your class.

Removing Obstacles to Serving God

Ancient people believed that if you actually saw God you would die. Isaiah cries out that he is "a man of unclean lips" (that is, a sinner). He confesses his own guilt and then adds that his people are also guilty of sin.

Talk with the other class members about things that you as a group do that may displease God. Include in your discussion, actions you take and attitudes you hold that you believe God does not like. Also include behaviors and attitudes that God would approve of but that you do not demonstrate. What changes do you need to ask God to help you make?

Responding To the Call

After Isaiah confessed his sin and received forgiveness (as symbolized by the angel touching his lips with the purifying fire of the burning coal), he was ready and able to respond to God's call. God is still calling people to speak prophetic words. God also needs people to go as missionaries, to be peacemakers, to speak a word of witness, to feed the hungry, to heal the sick, to teach, to listen with compassion, to organize and administer the work of the church, and on and on.

Sometimes God's call is for lifelong work. At other times, God speaks to people to ask them to do a certain task at a certain time. For example, members of one youth Sunday school class felt that God wanted them to help a woman and her three children after fire destroyed their home a few weeks before Christmas. Another group felt God calling them to work with Habitat for Humanity to build a home for a family in need. What might God be calling you and your classmates to do right now? What is your answer to God?

Wheeling Along the Scenic Route

Isaiah so vividly relates his encounter with God that you can see, hear, smell, touch, and taste what is happening. In each of the boxes below, draw or write what you imagine is being described in verses 1-4 and 5-8.

Isaiah 6:1-4	Isaiah 6:5-8

Reflecting On the Journey

God called Isaiah because the people were acting unjustly toward others, especially the poor. Isaiah knew that they—and he—were sinful people. Think about your own school, community, and church. Are people behaving in ways that you know are displeasing to God? What might God be calling you to do or say in some of these situations? What is your response to God? What will you actually do? You may want to record your thoughts in the space below.

The picture that Isaiah paints for the reader includes a vivid portrait of seraphs. These are angels who each have three pairs of wings. They are shown in Isaiah 6 as worshiping and serving God. What do you believe about angels? Do you think (or know) that you have somehow been touched by an angel? Record your experience.

Isaiah panicked when he realized that he could see God, because he knew he was a sinner. Instead of killing Isaiah, as ancient people thought would happen, God had the angels purify Isaiah's lips as an act of forgiveness. What words or actions do you need forgiveness for? Tell God how you have fallen short and offer a prayer for forgiveness. Be assured that God does forgive you. If possible, also ask forgiveness from the person or persons hurt by your unkind words or actions.

Perhaps you think that God calls only certain people to do God's work, while everyone else just watches or helps out once in awhile. That is not the case. God calls each and every Christian to speak in some way for God. Think of one person you could speak with about God this week and then do it.

This traditional South African hymn, known as "Thuma Mina," is based on Isaiah 6:8. Each verse begins with a call by a leader that all the other singers echo.

Send Me, Lord

WORDS: Traditional South African (Is. 6: 8)
MUSIC: Traditional South African
© 1984 Utryck
Used by permission of Walton Music Corporation.

Before you, Holy One, we are people of unclean lips and hearts. Touch us with the fire of your love, that we might praise you worthily. Speak your call to us, and give us courage to respond, "We will!" Show us your way, that we may walk in paths of goodness and truth, through the grace of Jesus Christ and the power of the Holy Spirit. Amen.[1]

---

[1] Prayer by Ruth C. Duck. Quoted in *Touch Holiness: Resources for Worship*, edited by Ruth C. Duck and Maren C. Tirabassi (The Pilgrim Press, 1990); page 49. Used by permission.

A New Covenant

"This is the covenant that I will make
with the house of Israel after those days,
says the LORD: I will put my law
within them, and I will write it on their hearts;
and I will be their God, and they
shall be my people."

(Jeremiah 31:33)

Searching For...

> ➤ an awareness of how the people broke the covenant God had made with them through Moses;
> ➤ why God planned to offer the people a new covenant;
> ➤ ways that I can know God in my own heart;
> ➤ I also want to know . . .

Setting Out on the Journey

1. Read Jeremiah 31:31-34.
2. Read or review the lesson on the Ten Commandments from Deuteronomy 5:1-21 (pages 21–26) to recall the covenant God made with the people through Moses.
3. How do you think this new covenant that Jeremiah speaks of might change the relationship between humans and God?

Getting Your Bearings

Look again at Jeremiah 31:31-34 to see how it points you in these directions:

➤ God had made covenants with the people of Israel, which they broke.
➤ God will not give up on the people but will make a new covenant with them.
➤ This new covenant will not be etched on two tablets of stone, as the one with Moses was, but will be written within people's hearts.
➤ Christians believe that this new covenant has been fulfilled through a relationship with Jesus Christ.

Exploring the Past

After God had led the people out of Egypt, God made a covenant with them at Mount Sinai in about 1250 B.C. The Ten Commandments are at the core of this covenant. Although the people agreed to what God had said, they soon disobeyed. In fact, the people were worshiping a golden idol shaped like a calf while Moses was on the mountain talking with God.

Things only got worse. Although God had said that the people were to worship no other gods, they regularly made and worshiped idols just like the ones their foreign neighbors worshiped. God was patient and forgiving for centuries. God sent prophets to warn the people that they would be punished if they didn't turn aside from their evil ways. Sometimes the people did repent—at least for a while. Most of the time, they did whatever they wanted, thinking that God would not let anything happen to them.

In 722 B.C., God allowed the Assyrians to wipe out what is called the Northern Kingdom or Israel. The people in the Southern Kingdom, also known as Judah, should have learned a lesson; but they didn't. By the time Jeremiah became a prophet in 626 B.C., people were still worshiping other gods, taking advantage of poor people, and doing other things that God had forbidden in the covenant with Moses. Jeremiah tells them that they have broken God's covenant. Through Jeremiah, the Judeans are reminded of God's desire to be in a loving relationship with them. This relationship will not be engraved on stone tablets but written on the hearts of God's people. Consider what that promise meant to those who first heard it.

Covenanting Together

Does your class or youth group have a covenant that helps members know what is expected of them and what they can expect from one another? If you already have a covenant, you may want to review it and make changes. If you do not have such an agreement, here are some questions that you might use to create one. You may want to look through your hymnal for references concerning covenant (or you can read the quotation from *The United Methodist Hymnal* that is found on the next page).

1. What behaviors will we expect?
2. What attitudes will we expect?
3. What actions will we take to invite others into our group and to help them feel included?
4. How will we handle situations when group members act in ways that violate our agreement?

After the group has reached agreement about what is to be included, write the covenant on paper and invite everyone to sign the covenant.

Bad News/Good News

God called Jeremiah to be a spokesperson. Much of the news he had to tell the people of Judah was bad: They had sinned and had broken God's covenant. God was going to punish them severely if they didn't shape up. Not all the news is bad, however. God is going to write the law *within their hearts* and forgive them. That is great news!

Suppose you and your group were called by God to point out ways in which God's people had sinned.

1. What would you say about how people are acting and talking in ways that are not in keeping with what we know God expects?
2. What would you tell people about God's love for them?
3. How would you describe a relationship with God based on the new covenant?
4. What would you say about Jesus and his place in your own life and heart?

covenant (COV-e-nant)—a binding written agreement between two or more parties; God's promise to humanity that includes God's blessings for those who obey and warnings of punishment for those who disobey

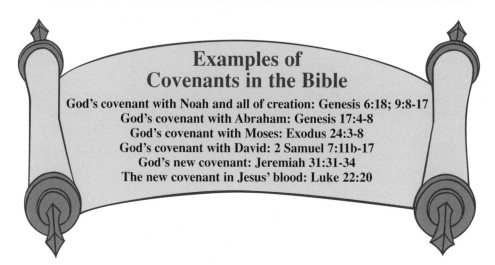

Examples of Covenants in the Bible

God's covenant with Noah and all of creation: Genesis 6:18; 9:8-17
God's covenant with Abraham: Genesis 17:4-8
God's covenant with Moses: Exodus 24:3-8
God's covenant with David: 2 Samuel 7:11b-17
God's new covenant: Jeremiah 31:31-34
The new covenant in Jesus' blood: Luke 22:20

Renewal of a Covenant

In Joshua 24:1-28, Joshua calls the people to renew their covenant with God. Joshua leads the way in verse 15 by saying that he and his household choose to serve God. The people respond in verse 18 by saying that they too will serve the Lord.

You may have an opportunity to renew your own covenant with God as part of your church's baptismal covenant. For example, when a person is baptized in a United Methodist church, the congregation responds with these words:

> **We give thanks for all that God has already given you**
> **and we welcome you in Christian love.**
> **As members together with you**
> **in the body of Christ**
> **and in this congregation**
> **of The United Methodist Church,**
> **we renew our covenant**
> **faithfully to participate**
> **in the ministries of the church**
> **by our prayers, our presence,**
> **our gifts, and our service,**
> **that in everything God may be glorified**
> **through Jesus Christ.** [1]

The covenants in the Bible are all initiated by God. People can choose to accept them or reject them, but they cannot change what God has said will be in the covenant. After people accept God's covenant, they can obediently keep it, knowing that God will bless them; or they can break it, knowing that God has reason to punish them. Of course, God often forgave people many times before finally punishing them. If you were God, how would you feel if people had said yes to your covenant and then went back on their word, even though you loved them and cared for them? In the space below, write some words or phrases to describe your feelings.

Jeremiah 31:34 says that God not only forgives sin but also does not even remember that sin. How does that make you feel? Write a few words that describe your feeling.

Suppose that you could write your own covenant with God. What behaviors and attitudes would you promise to observe? As a Christian, you might promise to be more respectful of your parents, or treat your siblings better, or steer clear of alcohol and other drugs, or wait until marriage to have sex. Write down several things that you will do, not because a written law says that you must do them, but because your relationship with God through Jesus is such a loving one that you make these promises *from your heart*.

LEADER: In truth and love, God has called us into this house of worship. God has said to us:

PEOPLE: "You are my people, I am your God."

LEADER: Not once, but again and again the Word is spoken, and there is rejoicing over all the earth. The words ring out with a glad cry:

PEOPLE: "You are my people, I am your God. You are my people, close to my heart."

LEADER: Come, O people of God; let us be glad as we sing God's praises; for our Creator and Redeemer has said:

PEOPLE: "You are my people, I am your God. You are my people, close to my heart."

LEADER: With awe and wonder, in the spirit of grace we lift our voices unto the God of creation, who redeems us and keeps us by the power of grace which comes from the God we worship this day. [2]

---

[1] From "Commendation and Welcome," in *The United Methodist Hymnal* (copyright © 1989 The United Methodist Publishing House); 43. Used by permission.
[2] Litany by Bonnie Jones-Witthun, from *Flames of the Spirit*, edited by Ruth C. Duck (Pilgrim Press, 1985); pages 66–67. Used by permission.

What Does the Lord Require of You?

What does the LORD require of you / but to
do justice, and to love kindness, / and to
walk humbly with your God?

(Micah 6:8)

Searching For...

> ➤ a better understanding of what God expects of humans;
> ➤ ways that God's people fail to live up to these expectations, both in the days of
>   Micah and today;
> ➤ ways that the words of a prophet who lived about seven hundred years before
>   Jesus affect my life today;
> ➤ I also want to know . . .

Setting Out on the Journey

1. Before you read Micah 6:6-8, jot down three things that you think God expects of
   you:

2. Now read the Bible verses. Compare your answers with the words of the prophet.
3. If you and your youth group were to take Micah's words seriously, what would you
   need to do differently?

Getting Your Bearings

Review Micah 6:6-8 to see how it points you in these directions:

➤ A worshiper wants to know what to bring before God.
➤ The prophet Micah answers that God is interested in people's behavior and attitudes, not specific offerings.
➤ God's people are to act with justice and to show love, mercy, and kindness to others.
➤ The people are also to walk obediently with God.

Exploring the Past

Micah was a prophet, a spokesperson for God, who came from a town in the Southern Kingdom (Judah) called Moresheth. He began prophesying about 725 B.C., just shortly before what was called the Northern Kingdom was overrun by an army from Assyria. According to 2 Kings 17:7-18, God let the Assyrians defeat the people because they worshiped other gods and disobeyed God's commandments. This military defeat was their punishment.

Although the Southern Kingdom where Micah lived survived, the prophet saw that the people of Judah and its capital city, Jerusalem, were just as disobedient as the people in the north had been. Micah spoke out against the people's failure to worship God faithfully and their injustices toward one another. For example, powerful people robbed and cheated the poor. Their actions stood in clear violation of God's commandments.

The Northern Kingdom had already been defeated. Micah prophesied that the Southern Kingdom would be punished as well. Jerusalem would be especially hard hit. While the religious leaders there were careful to make sure that the people followed all the right procedures for worship, they let injustices go unchecked. Micah's calls for social justice are similar to those of Amos, Hosea, and Isaiah. These prophets all understood that justice, lovingkindness, and obedience are requirements by which God's people are expected to live.

ESSENTIAL BIBLE PASSAGES FOR YOUTH

Pulling Together

It's Not Fair!

Read the following scenarios and decide what, if anything, seems to be unfair in each situation. Who is receiving unjust treatment? Why do you think this person or group is being treated unfairly? If you and your group could step into the situation, what would you do to overcome the injustice?

➤ "I'm really burned up," Matt fumed. "I was on the interstate driving home from work when a police car appeared out of nowhere and signaled me to pull over. The state trooper said I was doing ten miles over the speed limit and then gave me a ticket. Maybe I was, but lots of cars were passing me. I bet that cop was just jealous of a high school kid driving a red convertible."

➤ "I didn't do it, Mr. Thompson," pleaded Carlos. "Honest. Most of my teachers like me, but Ms. Jackson is always picking on me because I'm from another country. I did get into trouble once before, like most of the kids around here do. But I didn't start that fight in the hall. I just happened to be standing nearby and got the blame for it."

➤ "I was really surprised when I did the price comparisons you assigned us, Mrs. Cox," exclaimed Jenna. "I had no idea that people in the inner city pay so much more for food than we do here in the suburbs. What shocked me most was that the same items were priced differently in stores in the same grocery chain."

Living God's Way

Reread Micah 6:6-8. Then brainstorm ideas for each of these three columns:

ways I / we can be obedient to God	ways I / we can show justice	ways I / we can show mercy and lovingkindness

What steps can you and your group take this week to put at least one idea from each column into practice this week?

Look at this list of injustices and sins that Micah spoke out against. Put a check mark by the ones that people still commit today. Do you think there is more or less injustice among God's people now than in the days of Micah? Defend your answer.

☐ People want someone else's property, so they take it (Micah 2:2).

☐ People steal clothes from others (Micah 2:8).

☐ People cheat children out of their inheritance (Micah 2:9).

☐ Rulers know right from wrong, but they prefer to do what's wrong (Micah 3:1-2).

☐ Prophets lie, saying whatever people want to hear (Micah 3:5).

☐ Cruelty and murder are a way of life (Micah 3:9-10).

☐ Leaders and judges accept bribes (Micah 3:11; 7:3).

☐ Religious leaders teach and preach only for money (Micah 3:11).

☐ People practice witchcraft (Micah 5:12).

☐ People worship idols (Micah 5:13).

☐ Businesspersons cheat customers by using dishonest scales (Micah 6:10).

☐ Rich people are violent (Micah 6:12).

☐ Everyone lies (Micah 6:12).

☐ No one is loyal to God (Micah 7:2).

☐ People work together to commit crimes (Micah 7:3).

☐ Members of families rebel against and act disrespectfully toward one another (Micah 7:6).

What other injustices do you think exist today? List them in the space below.

Reflecting On the Journey

Read the following prayer by Basil the Great, who founded a monastery in the fourth century. Basil was known for his care of the sick and others in need. He was also a champion of poor people. Let this prayer help you think about how you act with justice and lovingkindness.

> The bread which you do not use
> Is the bread of the hungry.
> The garment hanging in your wardrobe
> Is the garment of one who is naked.
> The shoes that you do not wear
> Are the shoes of one who is barefoot.
> The money you keep locked away
> Is the money of the poor.
> The acts of charity you do not perform
> Are so many injustices you commit. [1]

If God were to speak through a prophet right now, what injustices do you think God would point out in your own community or school? What steps can the residents or students take right now to correct this unfairness? List these items below.

What does God want you to do right now to show justice and lovingkindness to others? Write your thoughts in the space below.

The World Methodist Social Affirmation

We believe in God, creator of the world and of all people;
　and in Jesus Christ, incarnate among us,
　　who died and rose again;
　and in the Holy Spirit,
　　present with us to guide, strengthen, and comfort.

We believe;
God, help our unbelief.

We rejoice in every sign of God's kingdom:
　in the upholding of human dignity and community;
　in every expression of love, justice, and reconciliation;
　in each act of self-giving on behalf of others;
　in the abundance of God's gifts
　　entrusted to us so that all may have enough;
　in all responsible use of the earth's resources.

Glory be to God on high;
and on earth, peace.

We confess our sin, individual and collective,
　by silence or action:
　　through the violation of human dignity
　　　based on race, class, age, sex, nation, or faith;
　　through the exploitation of people
　　　because of greed and indifference;
　　through the misuse of power
　　　in personal, communal, national, and international life;
　　through the search for security
　　　by those military and economic forces
　　　that threaten human existence;
　　through the abuse of technology
　　　which endangers the earth and all life upon it.

Lord, have mercy;
Christ, have mercy;
Lord, have mercy.

We commit ourselves individually and as a community
　to the way of Christ:
　　to take up the cross;
　　to seek abundant life for all humanity;
　　to struggle for peace with justice and freedom;
　　to risk ourselves in faith, hope, and love,
　　　praying that God's kingdom may come.

Thy kingdom come on earth as it is in heaven. Amen. [2]

---

[1] Quoted in *Praying with Hildegard of Bingen*, by Gloria Durka (Saint Mary's Press, 1991); page 50. Used by permission.
[2] Text © 1986 World Methodist Council. Quoted in *The United Methodist Hymnal* (Copyright © 1989 The United Methodist Publishing House); 886. Used by permission.

　　　　　　　　　　　　　　　　　　　ESSENTIAL BIBLE PASSAGES FOR YOUTH

Good News of Great Joy

The angel said to [the shepherds],
"Do not be afraid; for see—I am bringing you
good news of great joy for all the people:
to you is born this day in the city of David a Savior,
who is the Messiah, the Lord."

(Luke 2:10-11)

Searching For...

> ➤ an understanding of what the angel's message meant to the shepherds
> ➤ how the shepherds responded to the announcement of the birth of a Savior
> ➤ ways I can respond to this good news of great joy
> ➤ I also want to know . . .

Setting Out on the Journey

1. Read Luke 2:1-20.
2. Imagine that you are a TV reporter on the scene. What questions would you ask the shepherds? What questions would you ask the angel?

3. What photos would you ask the camera crew to take?

Getting Your Bearings

Review Luke 2:1-20 to see how it points you in these directions:

➤ Joseph and Mary had to leave their home in Nazareth to go to Joseph's hometown, Bethlehem, in order to be counted in a census ordered by the Roman emperor Augustus.
➤ Jesus' birth was first announced to shepherds.
➤ The angel tells the shepherds that Jesus is the Savior, Messiah, and Lord.
➤ The shepherds respond to the angel's news by going to visit Jesus and then telling others about what they had witnessed.

Exploring the Past

Luke records that Joseph and his fiancée Mary had left Nazareth to go to Bethlehem just before her baby was born. The emperor Augustus, who ruled from 27 B.C. to A.D. 14, had ordered a census so that everyone could be taxed. While scholars question the accuracy of Luke's date for the census, his story does help the reader understand why a couple would go on a journey just before the birth of a child. Just as important, Jesus' birth in Bethlehem fulfills a prophecy made by Micah (5:2).

As Luke 2:7 states, upon Jesus' birth, Mary placed him in a manger (or feeding trough) because the inn was filled. Everyone from Bethlehem would have been required to return home for the census, which would explain the crowd. The stable with its manger may have been located underneath the inn, for animals were often kept in a lower level of a home.

Though Mary, Joseph, and the new baby would have been unnoticed by others, an angel appeared to shepherds to announce the birth of a Savior, the Messiah, the Lord. The shepherds, who had been going about their ordinary business, responded to this astonishing news first with fear and then with action. They went to find the baby. Then they told others what the angel had said to them. Like the chorus of angels in heaven, the shepherds also praised and worshiped God for this matchless gift of Jesus. Their lives had been changed by this "good news of great joy."

ESSENTIAL BIBLE PASSAGES FOR YOUTH

Pulling Together

Announcements

People often send out announcements of events such as births, weddings, graduations, moving to a new home, or accepting a new job. Usually these announcements are written or printed on paper. Some people may send cassette tapes or videos or use some other creative way to let friends and family know about an important change in their life. God sent an angel to proclaim the important news of Jesus' birth.

Suppose you and your youth group were responsible for reporting to the world the news that Jesus is a Savior, the Messiah, the Lord. What would you do? Think of the most creative, exciting way possible to publicize this news.

Merry Christmas!

When the shepherds heard the news from the angel of the birth of the Savior, they rushed to find the baby Jesus and worship him. In our day, the most common sounds at Christmastime are likely to be cash registers jingling as shoppers rush to buy gifts.

How do you think God might feel about the way modern Christians in developed countries such as the US celebrate Christmas?

What ideas do you have for celebrating Christmas in ways that are more in keeping with the simple, worshipful response of the shepherds? How could you and your youth group work together to make such a Christmas happen?

Making Room for Others

Joseph and Mary had to go to a stable because there was no room for them at the inn. While the hotels, motels, and inns of our day may have plenty of space for guests, there are still many people who are not welcomed in our society at large.

Think about the kinds of people who may not be welcomed. These may include persons infected with HIV/AIDS, or drug addicts, or the homeless, or immigrants. What can you and your classmates do to make at least one person feel welcome and wanted? How would your action announce God's love to that person?

The Sounds of Christmas

Many familiar Christmas carols refer to the shepherds and the angels. See if you can identify the carols from which these words were taken. Write the name of the carol above each carol number.

Carol 1:

Angels we have heard on high
sweetly singing o'er the plains,
and the mountains in reply
echoing their joyous strains.
Gloria, in excelsis Deo!
Gloria, in excelsis Deo!

Carol 2:

Flocks were sleeping,
shepherds keeping
vigil till the morning new
saw the glory,
heard the story,
tidings of a gospel true.
Thus rejoicing,
free from sorrow,
praises voicing,
greet the morrow;
Christ the babe was born for you.

Carol 3:

Sing, choirs of angels,
sing in exultation;
O sing, all ye citizens of heaven above!
Glory to God,
all glory in the highest;
O come, let us adore him,
O come, let us adore him,
O come, let us adore him,
Christ the Lord.

Answers: 1. "Angels We Have Heard on High" (verse 1); 2. "Infant Holy, Infant Lowly" (verse 2); 3. "O Come, All Ye Faithful" (verse 3)

Picture yourself going about your regular business. Maybe you are sitting in a class-room, or working at a store in the mall, or helping with chores around the farm. Suddenly, an angel tells you the best news imaginable. A Savior—the Messiah (which also means anointed one or Christ) and the Lord—has been born nearby. How would you react to this news? Why would you go, or not go, to find the child? Who would you tell about your experience after you found the child? You may meditate on these ideas or write your thoughts in the space below.

Now imagine yourself as Mary. You are probably a teenager. You are engaged but not married, and now you have a baby. Before Jesus' birth the angel Gabriel appeared to you and told you that you were to bear the "Son of the Most High" (Luke 1:26-32). Shortly after Jesus' birth, some shepherds came and said to you that an angel had also told them about this child. You treasure the shepherds' words and keep them in your heart. What are you thinking? What are your hopes and dreams for this child?

Think about the angel's words in Luke 2:10-11. What difference has it made to the world that Jesus was born in Bethlehem almost two thousand years ago? What differ-ence has his birth made in your life?

Christ Is Born

WORDS: Traditional Byzantine Christmas prayer
MUSIC: Raquel Mora Martínez
From *The United Methodist Book of Worship.*
Copyright © 1992 by Abingdon Press

The music for this hymn lends itself to the use of instruments such as congo drums, maracas, and claves. The words may be sung either in unison or with one group acting as the leader and another group responding. Or everyone may say the words prayerfully in unison.

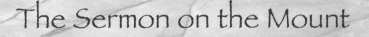

The Sermon on the Mount

When Jesus saw the crowds, he went up the
mountain; and after he sat down,
his disciples came to him.
Then he began to speak, and taught them.

(Matthew 5:1)

Searching For...

> ➤ the meaning of the Beatitudes and other parts of the Sermon on the Mount;
> ➤ why the things that Jesus taught would have been important to the people who heard him;
> ➤ how Jesus' teachings affect my life;
> ➤ I also want to know . . .

Setting Out on the Journey

1. Make a list of at least five experiences or things that, if you had them, would make you feel blessed by God.

2. Read Matthew 5:1-20. The word *blessed* may also be translated as "happy." How does your list compare with Jesus' list?

3. Had you been on that hillside with the disciples, what would you have wanted Jesus to explain more thoroughly to you?

Getting Your Bearings

Look again at Matthew 5:1-20 to see how it points you in these directions:

➤ In the Sermon on the Mount, Jesus teaches people how to live in the kingdom of God.
➤ Those who live according to Jesus' teachings will be happy and blessed.
➤ Jesus says that his followers will be persecuted, just as the prophets were.
➤ Jesus compares his followers to salt that gives flavor and light that shines for the world to see.

Exploring the Past

In Chapters 5–7 of his Gospel, Matthew records a collection of Jesus' teachings that Christians call the Sermon on the Mount. In this sermon, Jesus introduces key ideas concerning life in the kingdom of God, which Jesus himself is ushering in. Jesus makes clear that his teachings are not replacing God's law but fulfilling it.

The sermon begins in Matthew 5:3-11 with teachings known as the Beatitudes. Each verse begins with a word that in some Bible versions is translated as "blessed," while others say "happy." Jesus states that those who are happy are poor in spirit, grieving, meek, hungering for holiness, merciful, pure in heart, peacemakers, and persecuted. These are the ones who will be blessed by God. How strange Jesus' list of happy people sounds! His message runs counter to modern society's teaching that people who are happy are rich, powerful, successful, and liked by everyone. As is so often the case, Jesus' teaching is the exact opposite of what most people expect.

Jesus goes on in verses 13 and 14 to speak about his followers as salt and light. Salt was an important staple in Jesus' day. People used it not only to season their food but also to preserve it. If salt lost its flavor, or perhaps dissolved in water, it was no longer any good. Similarly, a candle had to be set where all could see it, not hidden under a basket, if it were to light the way for others. Jesus' disciples needed to let their own lives and their witness shine forth and give flavor to the lives of those around them.

Pulling Together

Happiness Is . . .

What does the world tell you is necessary for happiness? Can you be happy only if you use the right toothpaste, wear the right jeans, drive the right car, prepare for a certain job? Where do you get your information about the world's definition of happiness? Do your ideas come from TV programs, ads, your friends, your family, or from somewhere else? Take some time to examine these messages and their impact on your thinking and actions. How do they stand in contrast to Jesus' definition of happiness as found in the Beatitudes?

Persecuted for Who You Are

People in the early church were well aware that it would cost them something—perhaps even their life—to say that they were followers of Jesus. Religious persecution still exists around the world, though if you live in the United States or Canada you probably have not experienced it. Or have you? Read the following scenarios. What would you have done in each case?

Scenario 1: Robin and Alberto were asked to lead next week's youth program at church. They brought their Bibles and some other resources with them to school. During lunch, as they were making their plans and checking their materials for ideas, a classmate came up to them and asked, "Are you two Jesus freaks or something?" How would you have replied?

Scenario 2: The basketball team at Valley High had a shot at the league championship, especially if they could improve some of their plays. The coach called extra practices for Sunday nights for the next month. Eric was one of the star players; but he was also the president of his church's youth group, which met every Sunday night. The coach and the team members put pressure on Eric to be at practice. If you were Eric, what would you have done?

The Kingdom of God

Jesus taught the Beatitudes to the people who had gathered at the mountain to hear him. He wanted them to know what life in the kingdom of God would be like and how people who wanted to live under God's rule should conduct themselves. What changes would you and your youth group need to make to live according to Jesus' teachings? Do you think it is possible for you to live as Jesus taught? Why or why not?

Wheeling Along the Scenic Route

Blessed Are the Peacemakers

When Jesus refers to peacemakers in Matthew 5:9, he isn't just talking about people who stay out of arguments with others. He's referring to people who get involved in a difficult situation and work to bring about peace. Remember that Jesus would have understood peace to mean more than "the absence of conflict." The Hebrew word *shalom* means peace, health, wholeness, and harmony as God intended. Here are some people who have tried to bring about peace in their own way:

MARTIN LUTHER KING, JR.

A Baptist pastor, Dr. King believed that all people were equal in God's sight. Although he worked hard to bring about civil rights by means of peaceful protest, Dr. King was assassinated in Memphis in 1968.

MOTHER TERESA

An Albanian-born Roman Catholic nun, Mother Teresa works with her Missionaries of Charity in Calcutta and other places where there is suffering. She sees Christ in each person—the sick, the dying, the unlovely, the unloved.

DESMOND TUTU

An Anglican archbishop, Desmond Tutu worked to bring about peace and an end to apartheid (the legal separation of blacks and whites) in South Africa.

MILLARD FULLER

The founder of Habitat for Humanity International works tirelessly to create safe, affordable housing for working families with limited incomes. Habitat is a worldwide, ecumenical Christian movement.

Who do you know who tries to bring about peace? List one or more names in the space below. You may include yourself. Write a few words or draw a symbol to represent what this person does.

Reflecting On the Journey

Jesus says that his followers are to be the light of the world. Your witness and your good works give glory to God. How do you light the way toward God for other people? Are you a "shining example" of a faithful Christian disciple? If not, what changes do you need to make so that others can see God through you? You may want to write your thoughts in the space below.

Jesus says in Matthew 5:7, "Blessed are the merciful, for they will receive mercy." How do you express compassion for other people? Perhaps you are good at visiting friends when they are ill. Maybe you know just what to say to someone who is having problems. Perhaps you reach out to a classmate who is physically or mentally challenged and try to make that person feel accepted.

Think about some of the ways you show mercy and compassion toward others. Write your ideas in the space below. Try to think of additional ways you could demonstrate kindness and mercy. Perhaps the name of someone specific you could help will come to mind.

Jesus also teaches that those who mourn, or feel sorrowful, will be comforted and strengthened. Have you experienced the loss of a loved one? Are you mourning the loss of a relationship, even if the other person is not dead? If you have recently moved to a new location, do you feel grief because you are no longer with your friends? If you have felt any kind of loss, spend a few moments in silent prayer telling God of your sorrow and asking for comfort. If you prefer, write your prayer below.

The Beatitudes

[Group 1]: How blessed are the poor in spirit:

[Group 2]: the kingdom of Heaven is theirs.

[Group 1]: Blessed are *the gentle*:

[Group 2]: *they shall have the earth as inheritance.*

[Group 1]: Blessed are those who mourn:

[Group 2]: they shall be comforted.

[Group 1]: Blessed are those who hunger and thirst for uprightness:

[Group 2]: they shall have their fill.

[Group 1]: Blessed are the merciful:

[Group 2]: they shall have mercy shown to them.

[Group 1]: Blessed are the pure in heart:

[Group 2]: they shall see God.

[Group 1]: Blessed are the peacemakers:

[Group 2]: they shall be recognised as children of God.

[Group 1]: Blessed are those who are persecuted in the cause of uprightness:

[Group 2]: the kingdom of Heaven is theirs.

(Matthew 5:3-10, *The New Jerusalem Bible*) [1]

You are the salt of the earth.

You are the light of the world.

Pray This Way

"Pray then in this way: /
Our Father in heaven, /
hallowed be your name."

(Matthew 6:9)

Searching For...

> ➤ how the Lord's Prayer is a model for the way Christians are supposed to pray
> ➤ what this prayer shows me about God and what God expects of people
> ➤ the meaning of the Lord's Prayer in my own life
> ➤ I also want to know . . .

Setting Out on the Journey

1. Read Matthew 6:5-15.
2. Look carefully at the passage and decide how Matthew's version of the Lord's Prayer is similar to or different from the way you usually pray it.

3. Check several translations of the Bible. Look for the differences in the way they read. What new ideas do you get from these translations that help you understand Jesus' prayer more fully?

Getting Your Bearings

Reread Matthew 6:5-15 to see how that passage points you in these directions:

➤ Jesus explains that prayers are to be sincere.
➤ Jesus' prayer includes praise to God and petitions concerning God's kingdom.
➤ Jesus' prayer asks God for what humans need.
➤ Jesus' prayer encourages people to ask forgiveness from God and in turn to forgive others for the wrongs they have done.

Exploring the Past

The Lord's Prayer is found in a collection of Jesus' teachings known as the Sermon on the Mount. Scholars believe that Jesus offered this prayer in Aramaic, which was the everyday spoken language of the common people. Jesus' prayer was to serve as a model that would teach his disciples how to pray.

Before offering this model prayer, Jesus explained that God is displeased by certain attitudes such as hypocrisy. Some religious people of Jesus' day were obviously making a big show of their religion. Their purpose in praying was not to communicate with God but to let others see how religious they were. They wanted to be congratulated for their saintly behavior. Jesus made clear that God will not reward such prayers. God is not interested in hearing people drone on and on, making a big show of their piety. Notice that Jesus is not telling people that they cannot gather with others for prayer. Jesus himself prayed in the synagogue. Instead, he is speaking against an attitude that says "I'm holier than you."

After Jesus told the people about the kinds of prayers that God does not want to hear, Jesus prayed a model prayer for them. This familiar prayer has been said throughout Christian history in large church gatherings, as well as by persons praying alone in their rooms. The early church added the doxology with which Protestants close this beloved prayer: "For thine is the kingdom, and the power, and the glory, for ever."

Pulling Together

Your Kingdom Come, Your Will Be Done

Christians believe that God's kingdom is both present and yet to come. It is here in the sense that Jesus ushered in God's kingdom, but we have not yet experienced its fullness.

Here are some questions to discuss with someone else: What do you expect God's kingdom to be like? What will be different from what you experience now? What will be added? What will be taken away? How can doing God's will on earth help to bring about God's kingdom in its fullness? What are you actually praying for, then, when you pray for God's kingdom to come?

Forgive as You Are Forgiven

The teaching in Matthew 6:12 is difficult for many Christians to put into practice. You may find it easy to ask God to forgive you for your sins. But it's another matter for you to forgive someone else who has wronged you. Yet in verses 14-15, Jesus warns that we must be willing to forgive others if we expect to be forgiven by God.

Write a sentence prayer in which you ask God to forgive you for something you have done or left undone, as you forgive someone else who has done something against you. Be specific about what this other person has done to you.

Where Two or Three Are Gathered

In the Sermon on the Mount, Jesus teaches people about the kinds of things we should pray about. In Matthew 18:19-20, Jesus talks about God's openness to receiving our prayers. He says, "Again, truly I tell you, if two of you agree on earth about anything you ask, it will be done for you by my Father in heaven. For where two or three are gathered in my name, I am there among them."

Pray with your group about something everyone in the class wants. For example, you may want to experience world peace in your lifetime. You may want people across the globe to have their daily bread. You may want God to heal a rivalry between two groups or schools. Feel God's presence with you as you pray. Trust that your prayer will be answered in God's own way and time.

9 "Pray then in this way:
Our Father in heaven,
hallowed be your name.
10 Your kingdom come.
Your will be done,
    on earth as it is in heaven.
11 Give us this day our daily bread.
12 And forgive us our debts,
    as we also have forgiven our debtors.
13 And do not bring us to the time of trial,
    but rescue us from the evil one.

New Revised Standard Version

9 So you should pray like this:
Our Father in heaven,
may your name be held holy,
10 your kingdom come,
your will be done,
on earth as in heaven.
11 Give us today our daily bread.
12 And forgive us our debts,
as we have forgiven those who are in
debt to us.
13 And do not put us to the test,
but save us from the Evil One.

The New Jerusalem Bible

9 You should pray like this:
Our Father in heaven,
help us to honor your name.
10 Come and set up your kingdom,
so that everyone on earth will obey you,
    as you are obeyed in heaven.
11 Give us our food for today.
12 Forgive us for doing wrong,
    as we forgive others.
13 Keep us from being tempted
    and protect us from evil.

The Contemporary English Version

9 This, then, is how you should pray:
'Our Father in heaven;
    May your holy name be honored;
10 may your Kingdom come;
may your will be done on
    earth as it is in heaven.
11 Give us today the food we need.
12 Forgive us the wrongs we have done,
    as we forgive the wrongs
      that others have done to us.
13 Do not bring us to hard testing,
    but keep us safe from the Evil One.

Good News Bible: The Bible in
Today's English Version

9 After this manner therefore pray ye: Our Father which art in heaven,
Hallowed be thy name.
10 Thy kingdom come. Thy will be done in earth, as it is in heaven.
11 Give us this day our daily bread.
12 And forgive us our debts, as we forgive our debtors.
13 And lead us not into temptation, but deliver us from evil: For thine
is the kingdom, and the power, and the glory, for ever. Amen.

King James Version

Reflecting On the Journey

You have the privilege of praying to God, knowing that God will hear and answer you—though the answer may not be the one you wanted. Jesus has given you and all members of the community of faith a model prayer to show how prayer is to be offered. But do you pray each day? If you do not already have a devotional period, set aside ten minutes each day this week to pray. Conclude your time by saying the Lord's Prayer. Record any thoughts you have about daily prayer.

As long as you are not praying insincerely just to show others what a great Christian you are (see Matthew 6:5-8), the important thing about prayer is not how you pray but that you pray. Who or what do you need to pray for now? Begin this week to keep a prayer journal—a dated list of names of those for whom you have prayed, as well as a dated list of the responses and results. Remember that answers will come in God's time.

	WHO I PRAYED FOR	REASON	DATE ANSWERED
Sunday			
Monday			
Tuesday			
Wednesday			
Thursday			
Friday			
Saturday			

The Lord's Prayer

1. Our _____ Fa - ther, which art in heav - en,
2. Done on ___ earth as it is in heav - en,
3. And _____ for - give all ___ our debts, __
4. Lead ___ us not in - to ___ temp - ta - tion,
5. Thine is the king - dom, pow - er, and glo - ry,
6. A - men, a - men, __ a - men, __

hal - low - ed - a be thy name.

Thy
Give
As
—
A -

king - dom come, thy will be done, _____
us this day our dai - ly bread, _____
we for - give our debt - ors, _____
But de - liv - er us from e - vil,
For - ev - er and ev - er, _____
men, a - men, a - men, a - men, _____

Fine

hal - low - ed - a be thy name.

WORDS: Matthew 6:9-13; adapt. by J. Jefferson Cleveland and Verolga Nix, 1981
MUSIC: West Indian folk tune; arr. by Carlton R. Young, 1988
Adapt. © 1981 Abingdon Press; arr. © 1989 The United Methodist Publishing House

Rejoice With Me

" 'Rejoice with me, for I have found
the coin that I had lost.' Just so, I tell you,
there is joy in the presence
of the angels of God
over one sinner who repents."

(Luke 15:9b-10)

Searching For...

> an awareness of how God searches for those who are lost and wandering away from God;
> what these two parables in Luke might have meant to the tax collectors, sinners, Pharisees, and scribes to whom Jesus spoke;
> what these parables mean to me as I consider my own relationship with God;
> I also want to know . . .

Setting Out on the Journey

1. Read Luke 15:1-10.
2. Locate information on the different people in Jesus' audience: the tax collectors, sinners, Pharisees, and scribes.
3. Discover the point of the parables of the lost sheep and the lost coin. How do you think the different people in the audience would have reacted to the point of Jesus' stories? Why?

Getting Your Bearings

Review Luke 15:1-10 to see how it points you in these directions:

➤ The Pharisees and scribes were upset because Jesus willingly associated with people who did not live up to their understanding of the laws and teachings of the Jewish religion.
➤ Jesus' story about the lost sheep shows how far God the good shepherd will go to bring safely into the fold those who have wandered away.
➤ Jesus' parable about the lost coin makes the same point about God's diligence in searching for the lost.
➤ In both parables, God (reflected in the images of the shepherd and the homemaker) throws a party because what was lost has been found.

Exploring the Past

Wherever Jesus went, crowds came to be healed and to hear him teach. As Luke 15 opens, a crowd is gathering around Jesus. Some of the people in the crowd were looked down on by the religious leaders. Sinners included not only people who did bad things but also people who did not strictly obey all the Jewish rules. For example, someone who did not properly wash his or her hands before eating would be called a sinner. Tax collectors were also scorned by the leaders and by other Jews. The collectors often got rich because no rules governed their work. For instance, if a person owed one hundred dollars in taxes to the Roman government, the tax collector could charge him or her two hundred dollars and pocket an extra one hundred for himself.

The Pharisees and the scribes, who strictly followed Jewish laws, were quite upset by the fact that Jesus associated with people who were cheaters and law breakers.

To help all these different people understand what the kingdom of God was about, Jesus told two parables. (A parable may be simply defined as "an earthly story with a heavenly meaning.") In the parables in Luke 15:1-10 about a lost sheep and a lost coin, Jesus uses familiar words and everyday experiences to help the audience understand that God diligently seeks after everyone. God will not stop looking until the one who is lost is back in the fold.

Pulling Together

Inviting Others In

The purpose of Jesus' two parables in Luke 15:1-10 was to proclaim that God invites everyone into the Kingdom. All people are indeed welcome. Think about one or more persons you know who may not realize that Jesus is seeking them out and inviting them into the Kingdom. How can you invite these persons to join you in Sunday school, in worship, and/or in your youth group?

As a class, consider having a special "Bring a Friend Sunday" for the purpose of inviting friends to church who do not regularly attend. What could the class members do to make that day a special one? What could you personally do to make each guest feel so welcome that he or she may choose to attend regularly?

Consider having breakfast or refreshments. The group may also want to decorate the classroom with streamers or balloons. Decide how to go about contacting the guests after the event to thank them for coming and to invite them to come again.

Keeping Others Out

The religious leaders of Jesus' day were not that different from many modern church members. They had specific ideas about who God would—or would not—allow into the Kingdom. Jesus' parables about the sheep and the coin must have startled the Pharisees and the scribes. They thought they were doing God's will by keeping "undesirables" out. Jesus said that God was actually searching for such people, trying to bring them all into God's kingdom.

Think about ways your church in general or your class in particular may send messages to visitors that make them feel they are not welcome. Rate your class and yourself using the questions on the next page. Talk about how you and your group can be more open to inviting other people and helping them feel welcome when they arrive.

God's Choices

Suppose you were in charge of deciding who is "in" and who is "out" of the kingdom of God. Make a list describing the kinds of people you would let in, and another list describing those you would keep out. Now reread Luke 15:1-10. What do you think Jesus would say about your lists? What changes might he make?

Rating the Welcome Mat

Jesus taught that God is willing to do whatever is necessary to make sure that everyone is safely in God's fold. Christians understand this to mean that all people are invited to enter into a relationship with God through Jesus, and that all people are therefore to be included in the life of the church. But sometimes church members do a poor job of welcoming newcomers. Decide how much you agree or disagree with each statement below. Circle 1 if you strongly disagree, 2 if you disagree, 3 if you agree, and 4 if you strongly agree.

Most members of our class go out of their way to speak to a visitor.	1	2	3	4
We have no cliques in our class, so everyone feels free to join in.	1	2	3	4
Our teacher or group leader encourages us to bring friends.	1	2	3	4
People are willing to share supplies and books with visitors.	1	2	3	4
When I bring guests, I thank them for coming and invite them to come again.	1	2	3	4
People in my class try to encourage one another, rather than laughing at anyone for making a mistake.	1	2	3	4
We welcome newcomers regardless of their clothes or hairstyle.	1	2	3	4

Now rate your personal "welcome mat" by answering these questions:

How often do you invite someone to church or Sunday school?

    never   rarely   sometimes   often

How do you react to visitors or newcomers?

    ignore them   speak only if I know them   try to make them feel at home

If Jesus were to comment on your willingness to reach out to others and invite them into the church, write what you think he would say to you.

Reflecting On the Journey

Think about how you feel when you lose something important—really important. What emotions do you experience? The answer probably depends on what you have lost. If you were to misplace your report card, you might dread what your parents would say. If you lost a gift from a special friend, you would probably be upset because that treasure had sentimental value for you. If the lost item was an expensive musical instrument, you might worry about the cost of replacing it. If a pet happened to stray from home, you would probably grieve over the potential loss of a beloved friend.

Review the parables in Luke 15:1-10 and consider how you would have felt had you been the shepherd, the woman, and their friends. Write a few descriptive words or phrases in the space below.

Do you ever feel like that lost sheep? Perhaps you have wandered away from the rest of God's fold. Maybe the grass down the road looked greener. Maybe people seemed to be having more fun elsewhere. Regardless of the reason, you decided to distance yourself from God. Whether you know it or not, God is present with you and just waiting for you to say that you want to return. God will not force you to get back on track, but God and all the company of heaven will throw an awesome party if and when you decide to do that.

If you feel far from God, what prevents you from allowing God to find you? Imagine that God the good shepherd is standing over you, ready to pick you up and bring you home rejoicing. What would you say to God? What do you think God would say to you? You may want to write down your thoughts.

Seek, Find, Rejoice!

THE WOMAN: My coin was lost. I swept and cleaned and searched the house all over. The lost has now been found. Rejoice with me!

FRIENDS OF THE WOMAN: We share your joy and celebrate with you.

THE SHEPHERD: My sheep was lost. I trudged through the wilderness to find it before wild animals could devour the helpless creature. The lost is now safely in my arms. Rejoice with me!

FRIENDS OF THE SHEPHERD: We give thanks that you found the lost one that you risked your own life to save. We celebrate your successful search.

ALL THE FRIENDS: Tell us your secret. We too have lost things, but we never find them.

THE WOMAN AND THE SHEPHERD: Never give up! Never give up! Keep looking until the lost is found.

ALL THE FRIENDS: But that is hard. We grow tired and discouraged.

THE WOMAN AND THE SHEPHERD: Never give up! Never give up! Keep looking until the lost is found.

ALL THE FRIENDS: Why should we leave the others to search for one that is lost and may never be found?

THE WOMAN AND THE SHEPHERD: Never give up! Never give up! Keep looking until the lost is found. God seeks the lost—every one of them. And God never gives up.

ALL THE FRIENDS: You have shown us God's way. We will continue to search for those who are lost.

THE WOMAN AND THE SHEPHERD: And when the lost are found, we will rejoice with you. For God and the whole company of heaven rejoice when the one who was lost is found.

They Crucified Jesus

When they came to the place that is called
The Skull, they crucified Jesus there with the
criminals, one on his right and one on his left.
Then Jesus said, "Father, forgive them;
for they do not know what they are doing."

(Luke 23:33-34a)

Searching For...

> ➤ a sense of how the people who witnessed the Crucifixion responded to Jesus
> ➤ the importance of the Crucifixion in the life of the church
> ➤ what Jesus' crucifixion means in my own life
> ➤ I also want to know . . .

Setting Out on the Journey

1. Read Luke 23:26-47.
2. Try to put yourself in the place of each of the people in the story: Simon of Cyrene, the women, the criminals on the cross next to Jesus, the leaders, the soldiers, and the centurion. As each person, what did you think about Jesus? How did his death affect what you believed?

3. What difference would Jesus' words of forgiveness (verse 34) have made in your life?

Getting Your Bearings

Review Luke 23:26-47 to see how it points you in these directions:

➤ Jesus was crucified outside the city of Jerusalem at a place called The Skull.
➤ Many people witnessed Jesus' crucifixion.
➤ The Crucifixion had different meanings for different people.
➤ Jesus asked God to forgive the people who were crucifying him because they did not know what they were doing.

Exploring the Past

Although only Matthew and Luke write about Jesus' birth, all four of the Gospel writers include detailed accounts of the events leading up to the Crucifixion on the day that Christians call Good Friday.

Luke begins in 23:26 by relating the story of the walk to the place of crucifixion called The Skull or, as it was known in the Aramaic language of Jesus' day, Golgotha. Simon, who came from Cyrene in North Africa, was pressed into service to carry the cross behind Jesus. Such a thing was not unusual. Because persons condemned to crucifixion were usually weak from beatings, bystanders were often ordered to carry a cross to the place of crucifixion. Along the way, Jesus spoke to the women, the only people who were shedding tears over his death. He told them to cry for unbelieving Jerusalem instead. Jesus asked God to forgive the people responsible for his death because they were unaware of what they were actually doing.

Luke records that Jesus was crucified between two criminals. One of the criminals, the soldiers, and the leaders insulted Jesus, made fun of him, and told him to perform a miracle to save himself. In contrast, the other criminal wanted Jesus to remember him when he came into his kingdom. Jesus promised that he would do just that.

Darkness covered the earth for about three hours while Jesus was on the cross. Luke records another strange event: The curtain that separated the restricted area of the Holy of Holies from the rest of the Temple was torn in two. After that, Jesus put himself into God's hands and died. One of the Roman soldiers who had witnessed the Crucifixion realized that Jesus was innocent and praised God.

Pulling Together

We Were There

As you read the story of Jesus' crucifixion from Luke 23:26-47, you imagined your-self witnessing the event from the point of view of different characters in the story. The actual crucifixion can never be repeated, of course; but people today may view Jesus in ways similar to those in the original story.

(1) Simon of Cyrene takes up Jesus' cross and follows him. This is what Jesus expects of all his disciples, according to Luke 9:23: "If any want to become my followers, let them deny themselves and take up their cross daily and follow me." How can you and the other members of your youth group take up your own cross? What meaning does such a statement have in your life today?

(2) One of the criminals, the leaders, and the soldiers insulted Jesus and made fun of him. What do people in modern society do to insult and make fun of Jesus?

(3) The second criminal and the Roman centurion (soldier) had not believed in Jesus before the Crucifixion. Yet the criminal wanted to be with Jesus (23:42-43) and the sol-dier said that Jesus was innocent (23:47). Can you think of any desperate situations in which people end up puting their faith in God? Can you think of any specific persons (either friends or well-known people) who have turned their life over to Jesus because of a crisis? What happened?

Jesus' Work on the Cross

In his Gospel, Luke describes what happens to Jesus; but he does not tell us what it all means. However, other Bible writers, such as Paul, and people throughout Christian his-tory have helped us understand that the purpose of Jesus' death was to enable everyone to be put right with God. Jesus died so that we could have eternal life.

Work together to decide

(1) what this gift of Jesus' death on the cross means to you;

(2) what this gift means to your youth group and community of faith;

(3) how you as individuals and as a group can tell others who Jesus was, why he died, and that they are invited to enter into a relationship with God through Jesus.

The LATIN cross, formed by two straight lines that intersect, is the type of cross most often used.

The CALVARY cross has three steps beneath it that stand for faith, hope, and love. You may find this cross on the altar in your church's sanctuary.

The CELTIC cross was taken from what is now Ireland to the island of Iona in the Hebrides by Columba, a sixth-century missionary who started a monastery there.

The ANCHOR cross, which originated in Egypt, was used by Christians who met in the underground burial chambers known as catacombs.

The JERUSALEM or CRUSADER'S cross has four small crosses between the main arms of the cross. Together, they symbolize the five wounds of Jesus. Godfrey de Bouillon (c. 1058–1100) was elected the first ruler of Jerusalem after the Crusaders won the city in 1099.

The MALTESE cross, made of four spears that point toward one another, dates back to the time of the Crusades. The order of the Knights Hospitalers, also known as the Knights of Malta because they were headquartered on that island, made this cross their emblem.

The CROSS and CROWN, based on the words of Revelation 2:10, symbolizes the crown that those who are faithful to the crucified Jesus will receive in the life after death.

The CROSS and TRIANGLE is often found in needlework art in the church, such as altar cloths and kneelers. The triangle symbolizes Christ's part in the Trinity of Father, Son, and Holy Spirit.

The CROSS CROSSLET, composed of four Latin crosses that are joined, represents the spreading of Christianity to the four corners of the earth.

Read the following poem. Do you agree with the poet's last sentence? In the space that is provided, write a few words or sentences that describe what the cross means to you and how it affects your life.

Your Cross

by Dayalan Devanesen

When I think of Good Friday
I think of your cross.

Today I see crosses
In chapels and churches
Surmounting steeples
On altars.
Brass crosses. Silver crosses. Gold.
Some studded with jewels
All surrounded by walls.

When I think of Good Friday
I think of your cross.

It was out on the open highway
And stood between thieves.
Soldiers. Gamblers. Drunkards.
All sorts of people.

Suddenly I feel something is
wrong. [1]

When I Survey the Wondrous Cross

by Isaac Watts

When I survey the wondrous cross
on which the Prince of Glory died,
my richest gain I count but loss,
and pour contempt on all my pride.

Forbid it, Lord, that I should boast,
save in the death of Christ, my God;
all the vain things that charm me most,
I sacrifice them to this blood.

(Think about "the vain things that charm [you]
most" and then silently offer them to God.)

See, from his head, his hands, his feet,
sorrow and love flow mingled down.
Did e'er such love and sorrow meet,
or thorns compose so rich a crown?

Where the whole realm of nature mine,
that were an offering far too small;
love so amazing, so divine,
demands my soul, my life, my all.

(Silently think of what "[your] all" is.
Then think of what God may be demanding
from the group as a whole.)

[1] From *Gifts of Many Cultures: Worship Resources for the Global Community*, by Maren C. Tirabassi and Kathy Wonson Eddy (United Church Press, 1995); page 158. Used by permission.

Jesus Is Alive!

The angel said to the women,
"Do not be afraid; I know that
you are looking for Jesus who was crucified.
He is not here; for he has been raised,
as he said. Come, see the place where he lay."

(Matthew 28:5-6)

Searching For...

➤ a sense of what it must have been like to be present on Easter morning
➤ what the Easter events meant to Jesus' first followers
➤ what the story of the Resurrection means in my life
➤ I also want to know . . .

Setting Out on the Journey

1. Read Matthew 28:1-10.
2. Pretend that you are one of the women. How do you feel when the angel speaks to you? What do you think is happening? What do you say to the risen Christ when you first see him?

3. In a sentence or two, try to summarize what you believe about the Resurrection and how it affects your own life.

Getting Your Bearings

Review Matthew 28:1-10 to see how it points you in these directions:

➤ Jesus had died and was buried in a cave-like tomb, as was the custom in first-century Jerusalem.
➤ Several women went to the tomb on Sunday, the day after the Jewish sabbath, to mourn. They would likely perform appropriate burial rituals that could not be done on the sabbath.
➤ When the women arrived, an angel moved the stone that was in front of the tomb and announced Jesus' resurrection.
➤ As the women were on their way to tell the disciples what the angel said, they met and worshiped Jesus, who told them to tell the disciples to go to Galilee.

Exploring the Past

Beginning with the earliest followers, Jesus' resurrection has been the cornerstone of the Christian faith. The tomb was empty! God had raised the crucified Jesus from the dead. The women and the disciples (28:16-20) bore witness to the fact that Jesus was alive. Even the soldiers sent to guard the tomb had witnessed the scene between the angel and the women. However, according to Matthew's account, they were bribed by religious leaders to say that the body had been snatched by Jesus' followers (28:11-15).

Each of the four Gospels gives an account of the Resurrection, though the details in Matthew, Mark, Luke, and John differ. The point of the story—that Jesus is alive—is clearly evident in all the stories. In Matthew's version, only two women—Mary Magdalene and the other Mary—go to the tomb that Joseph of Arimathea had donated for Jesus. They arrive at dawn on Sunday morning. After an earthquake an angel moves the stone away from the entrance to the tomb. The angel comforts the fearful women, shows them the empty tomb, and announces that Jesus has risen. As the women hurry to tell the disciples that Jesus is alive, they meet the Lord on the road and worship him.

A Victory Celebration

The Resurrection brings new life in the present and hope for eternal life with God. Christians are called to rejoice in this great news, the true message of Easter. How can you and your classmates celebrate the resurrection of Jesus? Will you sing or dance? Perhaps you will participate in a roleplay of the story of the two women, the angel, and the resurrected Jesus. What can you personally do to celebrate the Easter event?

What Happened?

When the two Marys heard from the angel that Jesus had been raised from the dead, they "ran to tell his disciples" (Matthew 28:8). Suppose you had been one of the women. What, exactly, would you have told the disciples? Suppose you were one of the disciples. What would you have said to these women who insisted that Jesus is alive? Suppose you had been an outsider who happened to see what was going on. What would you ask the women? What would you think or believe about Jesus?

Jesus' Resurrection and the Church's Faith

Not everyone believed that Jesus had actually been raised from the dead. The soldiers guarding the tomb had been bribed, according to Matthew 28:11-15, to say that the disciples stole Jesus' body. Undoubtedly some people believed their false story. Others questioned whether someone who was dead and buried could actually be resurrected. According to Luke 24:41, even the disciples who saw Jesus could not at first believe it was he.

The apostle Paul deals with the importance of the Resurrection in 1 Corinthians 15:12-20. Here Paul argues that if Jesus was not indeed raised from the dead by God, then people's faith in Christ is useless. Paul says in no uncertain terms that Christ was indeed resurrected. The basis for the Christian faith—Jesus' resurrection—is for real!

Like some of the early skeptics, not all modern Christians firmly believe that Jesus was resurrected. They have nagging doubts. With one other person, talk about both your belief concerning the Resurrection and any questions you may have. Consider the importance of belief in the Resurrection in your own faith journey.

He Rose

They crucified my Savior and nailed him to the tree,
they crucified my Savior and nailed him to the tree,
they crucified my Savior and nailed him to the tree,
and the Lord will bear my spirit home.

(Refrain to be read or sung after each verse):

He rose, (he rose) he rose, (he rose)
he rose from the dead!
He rose, (he rose) he rose, (he rose)
he rose from the dead!
He rose, (he rose) he rose, (he rose)
he rose from the dead,
and the Lord will bear my spirit home.

Then Joseph begged his body and laid it in the tomb,
then Joseph begged his body and laid it in the tomb,
then Joseph begged his body and laid it in the tomb,
and the Lord will bear my spirit home.

Sister Mary she came running, a looking for my Lord,
Sister Mary she came running, a looking for my Lord,
Sister Mary she came running, a looking for my Lord,
and the Lord will bear my spirit home.

An angel came from heaven and rolled the stone away,
an angel came from heaven and rolled the stone away,
an angel came from heaven and rolled the stone away,
and the Lord will bear my spirit home. [*]

---

[*] You will find the music to this lively African American spiritual on page 316 of *The United Methodist Hymnal*. The hymn tells the story of Good Friday and Easter.

ESSENTIAL BIBLE PASSAGES FOR YOUTH

Read at least one of the other reports of the first Easter morning as found in Mark 16:1-8; Luke 24:1-12; and John 20:1-10. How is each one similar to or different from the account in Matthew 28:1-10? Which of the details seem especially meaningful or important to you? Which account do you prefer? Why? Why do you think the church has so carefully preserved all these accounts, rather than selecting one "official" record?

What difference does Jesus' resurrection make in your own life? What confidence or assurance do you have about God, based on God's ability to raise Jesus from the dead? If you could talk face-to-face with Jesus right now, what questions would you ask him about the Resurrection? Jot down those questions:

As the apostle Paul argued, if Jesus had not been resurrected from the dead, then no one else could be raised either. But Jesus was in fact resurrected. Therefore, all Christians have hope in eternal life. What do you think eternal life will be like? Write down any words or phrases that come to mind:

The butterfly is often seen as a symbol of resurrection and eternal life. Just as the butterfly leaves its cocoon with a new body and flies upward, so the resurrected Jesus and those who believe in him have new life.

(**Benediction**): "Now may the God of peace, who brought back from the dead our Lord Jesus, the great shepherd of the sheep, by the blood of the eternal covenant, make you complete in everything good so that you may do his will, working among us that which is pleasing in his sight, through Jesus Christ, to whom be the glory forever and ever. Amen" (Hebrews 13:20-21).

Filled With the Holy Spirit

When the day of Pentecost had come, they were all together in one place. And suddenly from heaven there came a sound like the rush of a violent wind, and it filled the entire house where they were sitting. Divided tongues, as of fire, appeared among them, and a tongue rested on each of them. All of them were filled with the Holy Spirit and began to speak in other languages, as the Spirit gave them ability.

(Acts 2:1-4)

Searching For...

> information about what happened on Pentecost when the Holy Spirit fell upon the disciples and empowered them for ministry;
> an understanding of how the coming of the Holy Spirit enabled the church to be born and begin to grow;
> a vision of what my own church can be and do;
> I also want to know . . .

Setting Out on the Journey

1. Read Acts 2:1-13 and 38-47.
2. Imagine the feel of the wind, the heat of the flame, and the sound of God being proclaimed in many languages at once.
3. Picture yourself as a member of the first church. How has your life changed since you repented and believed in Jesus? What do you and the other members do to grow as Jesus' followers?

Getting Your Bearings

Review Acts 2:1-13 and 38-47 to see how it points you in these directions:

➤ The disciples were gathered in Jerusalem awaiting the fulfillment of the promise that Jesus would send the Holy Spirit (Acts 1:8).
➤ Jerusalem was filled with Jews who had come to celebrate an important Jewish festival, Pentecost, which was observed seven weeks (about fifty days) after Passover.
➤ The people in Jerusalem had come from all parts of the Roman Empire and spoke different languages. They were amazed to hear God's greatness proclaimed in their own language by the disciples, who were all from Galilee and spoke only one language.
➤ Following a sermon by Peter, about three thousand people accepted Jesus, were baptized, and formed the early church.

Exploring the Past

The Acts of the Apostles was written by Luke as a sequel to his Gospel. The first history book of the church, Acts records the work of the disciples and others in spreading the good news of Jesus.

In Acts 1, the resurrected Jesus meets with the disciples before ascending into heaven. He tells them to wait in Jerusalem to receive the power of the Holy Spirit (verse 8). Once they have that power, they are to be his witnesses.

As Acts 2 begins, the disciples are keeping a low profile. They had seen Jesus crucified and were not eager to follow him to the cross. Yet, just as Jesus promised, the Holy Spirit did come upon them in such power that they could not do anything but tell others about what God had done. No one could question the Spirit's presence, for it came with a rush of wind and tongues of fire. The disciples could speak in languages that they had never learned so those who knew these languages could easily understand what was being said. The people who had packed into Jerusalem for the festival of Pentecost were bewildered by what was happening. Some thought the disciples were drunk. One of the disciples, Peter, gave a sermon in which he quoted a prophecy from Joel 2:28-32 about the coming of the Spirit. Peter spoke eloquently about Jesus. The listeners responded by repenting and being baptized. They formed the early church, a fellowship of believers who did many of the same things that modern church members do.

Pulling Together

Power From On High

Reread the story of the Spirit's descent in Acts 2:1-13. These words probably cannot begin to describe the scene as the Spirit came upon the disciples. Nor can they capture the emotions of the disciples, who knew the Spirit would come but had no idea what that would mean. Neither can these words truly express the shock that the Jews who heard God's greatness being proclaimed in their own languages must have experienced.

If you and your classmates were to produce a multimedia program about the events in Acts 2:1-13, what special effects would you use? How would your program help people feel that they were in Jerusalem on this miraculous day on which the church truly began?

Witnessing to Others

The Holy Spirit came upon the disciples in a miraculous way. The purpose of the Spirit's coming was to empower Jesus' followers to bear witness to him. In other words, they were to go out—unafraid and unashamed—and tell others about Jesus' life, teachings, crucifixion, and resurrection. The witnesses were to invite people to enter into a relationship with Jesus and thus enter the kingdom of God. Peter's sermon in Acts 2:14-40 is an example of the powerful kind of witness that a Spirit-empowered person can make.

Think about how you and the members of your class witness for Jesus. How does what you say encourage other people to come to Jesus? What do your actions say to others about how Jesus' followers live and relate to other people? What changes might you need to make to be more faithful, Spirit-led witnesses?

We Are the Church

Look at Acts 2:42-47. Make a list of the activities of the first church. Which of these activities happens in your church? Which ones happen in your class or youth group? What purpose does each of these types of activities serve? How do they help bring new people into the church? How do they help the people who are already there to grow so as to be more faithful followers of Jesus?

What are some symbols of Pentecost that you have seen? For example, the symbol of The United Methodist Church is the cross and the flame. You may have noticed this symbol posted on a church sign board or attached above the front door. Examine the cross and flame symbol or draw your own symbol for Pentecost. In the space provided, write your thoughts about what this symbol may mean. How does it relate to Jesus' crucifixion and resurrection? How does it remind you of Pentecost (see especially Acts 2:3)? What does the symbol say to you about the kind of church Christians are called to be?

Reflecting On the Journey

Read Acts 2:1-38. Suppose you had been one of the people who were in Jerusalem for the festival of Pentecost. You may never have heard of Jesus. Suddenly, unexplainable events occur that cause you to wonder what is going on. Then a man named Peter stands up and preaches convincingly about God's saving work in Jesus. What do you do? How do you respond?

If you have not said yes to Jesus in your own life, what does this reading from Acts prompt you to do? (You may want to record your thoughts.) Speak with your parents, teacher, counselor, or pastor if you have questions about your own relationship with Jesus.

Acts 2:42-47 tells what the members of the newly-formed church did. Which of these activities do you regularly participate in? Which ones do you do sometimes? Which ones have you never tried? How might this description of the first church challenge you to be a more committed, involved member of the church? You may want to jot down some ideas.

Peter—the same Peter who had denied Jesus just a few weeks before (see Luke 22:54-62)—spoke powerfully about God's work in Jesus and about how God had raised Jesus from the dead. In doing so, Peter was fulfilling Jesus' instructions in Acts 1:8 that his followers are to be witnesses to the ends of the earth. In what ways are you a witness? How do you let people know of God's mercy and love as the church has seen and experienced it in Jesus?

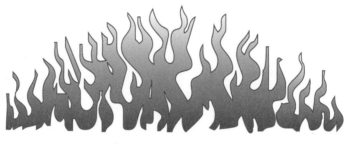

Pentecost Litany

by Jann C. Weaver

LEADER: Come, believers and faithful ones, sing your alleluias to God!

PEOPLE: Praise God, who invades us with the rush of a mighty wind and fills us with fire.

LEADER: Praise God, who out of love for us sent Jesus Christ to live among us.

PEOPLE: Praise God, whose spirit is poured out upon all flesh so our sons and daughters might prophesy.

LEADER: God reaches into our lives and claims us, calling us honored and loved.

PEOPLE: We are God's people: We are redeemed; for God has called us by name.

UNISON: Come, Holy Spirit, and find us in our wilderness. Lead us forth into the wonders of your love. [1]

(Blessing from 2 Corinthians 13:13): The grace of the Lord Jesus Christ, the love of God, and the communion of the Holy Spirit be with all of you. [Amen.]

---

[1] From *Flames of the Spirit*, edited by Ruth C. Duck (The Pilgrim Press, 1985); page 46. Used by permission.

One Body in Christ

For as in one body we have many members, and not all the members have the same function, so we, who are many, are one body in Christ, and individually we are members one of another. We have gifts that differ according to the grace given to us.

(Romans 12:4-6a)

Searching For...

> ➤ what it means to be one body in Christ
> ➤ the different types of gifts that God has given to members of the body of Christ
> ➤ the gifts that I have to contribute to the body of Christ
> ➤ I also want to know . . .

Setting Out on the Journey

1. Read Romans 12:3-8.
2. Write down the names of the members of your youth group or other people you know at church. Think of at least one gift or talent (for example, singing, listening, organizing an event) that each person (including you) has and write that gift next to the appropriate name.

3. Think of three things your group or church has been able to do because members willingly used their gifts.

Getting Your Bearings

Review Romans 12:3-8 to see how it points you in these directions:

➤ Paul uses the image of the body to remind Christians that all are joined together in Christ.
➤ Like the human body, the body of Christ has many parts, each of which has an important role to play.
➤ For the body of Christ to work properly, God has given members of the body different gifts, including the gift of prophecy, ministry, teaching, preaching, giving, leading, and compassion.
➤ Each member is expected to use the gift or gifts that he or she has been given so that the whole body will benefit.

Exploring the Past

The apostle Paul wrote to the church in Rome between A.D. 54 and 58. He had hoped to visit this church that was founded by others, so he wrote a letter telling them about the good news of God's salvation.

In Chapter 12, Paul explains his understanding of a holy life. He uses the image of a human body to help his readers see that each person—each member of the body—has an important and useful task to perform. Each one has been given gifts to build up the body, which is the church.

The church isn't like an amusement arcade where you can come and go whenever you want and enjoy a game with whoever happens to be there. Instead, each person has a specific role to play in the life of the church. God has given every person at least one gift. Because different people have different gifts, all members must participate and must use their gifts for the good of the whole body. Just as all parts of the human body must work together if the body is going to function effectively, so must all members of the body of Christ work in harmony with one another. As Paul writes, God has given the church gifts so that people can preach, teach, prophesy, show compassion, give generously, lead, and administer the work of the congregation.

Pulling Together

Everyone Has Gifts

Brainstorm a list of gifts that you feel help the church. If you get stuck, you'll find some ideas on the next page, as well as in 1 Corinthians 12:4-11, 28 and in Ephesians 4:11. Where would you put your own name on that list? Where would you put the name of each member of your class or youth group? If you are doing this activity with a group, were you surprised that people saw gifts in you that you didn't know you had? Did you learn about gifts that others have that you were not aware of? How are you using your gifts, both individually and together, for the benefit of the church? In what new ways could you use your gifts so as to build up the church even more?

Gifts for Living

If you are a middle school/junior high student, you may be taking a variety of courses in school that will help you discover who you are and what your special gifts may be. If you're a senior high student, you may have already identified things that you do well and that you may be thinking about using as a volunteer or in a career.

You may, for example, be a good listener who knows how to show compassion and make people feel comfortable even in a difficult situation. You could use your gifts in a health-related profession, in counseling or social work, or in the ordained ministry. Maybe you're the one who's always called on to lead the singing. Perhaps you could become a professional musician, a choir director, a volunteer choir member, a music teacher, or an actor in musical theater roles. Fill in these three columns and then answer the questions below:

My Interests	Talents I Think I Have	Talents Others Say I Have

What careers would combine your interests and your talents?

Who could help you find information about those careers and the training you would need to enter them?

How would you see yourself as being a faithful Christian disciple in these careers, whether or not they are related to the church?

I am part of the body of Christ, and I have gifts to share.

EARS
I am good at listening
to others.

MOUTH
I am good at expressing ideas
and sharing with others.

EYES
I am good at seeing the
needs of others.

BRAIN
I am good at planning
and organizing.

ARMS
I am good at reaching
out to others.

HANDS
I am good at doing the work
of the group.

HEART
I am good at planning
times of inspiration.

FEET
I am good at bringing people
to our group.[1]

Where do you fit into the body of Christ?

Read and meditate on the following words from a familiar hymn. The words are old, but the message is as important today as it was when it was written in 1873. What gifts has God given to you that you have offered back to God? What gifts could you use in God's service that you are not now using?

Take My Life, and Let It Be

by Frances R. Havergal

Take my life, and let it be
consecrated, Lord, to thee.
Take my moments and my days;
Let them flow in ceaseless praise.
Take my hands, and let them move
at the impulse of thy love.
Take my feet, and let them be
swift and beautiful for thee.

Take my voice, and let me sing
always, only, for my King.
Take my lips, and let them be
filled with messages from thee.
Take my silver and my gold;
not a mite would I withhold.
Take my intellect, and use
every power as thou shalt choose.

Take my will, and make it thine;
it shall be no longer mine.
Take my heart, it is thine own;
it shall be thy royal throne.
Take my love, my Lord, I pour
at thy feet its treasurestore.
Take myself, and I will be
ever, only, all for thee.

In the vacant places
We will build with new bricks
There are hands and machines
And clay for new brick
And lime for new mortar
Where the bricks are fallen
We will build with new stone
Where the beams are rotten
We will build with new timbers
Where the word is unspoken
We will build with new speech
There is work together
A Church for all
And a job for each
Every man to his work. [2]

What gifts has God given you to build the church?

How are you working together with others in the community of faith to build the church?

---

[1] From "Commitment Service: A Call to Discipleship," in *The United Methodist Youth Fellowship Handbook* (Copyright © 1989 by Discipleship Resources); page 207. Reprinted with permission from Discipleship Resources, Nashville, Tennessee.
[2] Excerpt from "Choruses From 'The Rock'" in COLLECTED POEMS 1909–1962, by T. S. Eliot (copyright 1936 by Harcourt Brace & Company, copyright © 1964, 1963 by T. S. Eliot); pages 149–50. Reprinted by permission of the publisher.

ESSENTIAL BIBLE PASSAGES FOR YOUTH

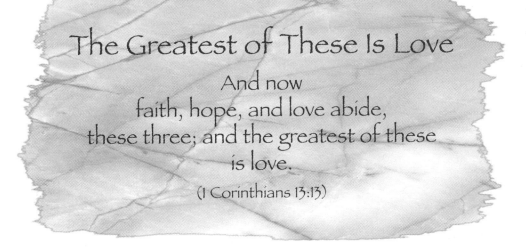

The Greatest of These Is Love

And now
faith, hope, and love abide,
these three; and the greatest of these
is love.

(1 Corinthians 13:13)

Searching For...

➤ the apostle Paul's teaching on the gift of love;
➤ an understanding of why love is so important;
➤ how loving others with the unselfish love that Paul writes about will make a difference in my life and in the life of others;
➤ I also want to know . . .

Setting Out on the Journey

1. Read 1 Corinthians 13:1-13.
2. How does Paul describe love? Try to state his ideas in your own words.

3. Imagine what the world would be like if people practiced the kind of love Paul describes. How, do you think, would the world be different?

Getting Your Bearings

Review 1 Corinthians 13:1-13 to see how it points you in these directions:

➤ No matter what spiritual gifts you seem to have, none of them is of any value unless you have love.
➤ Love is patient, kind, loyal, hopeful, trusting, and never-ending.
➤ Love is not jealous, boastful, proud, rude, selfish, or quick-tempered.
➤ Love will last.

Exploring the Past

According to Acts 18:1-11, Paul played an important role in establishing the church at Corinth, a major port city on the Greek peninsula. First Corinthians 16:8 indicates that Paul wrote this letter to the Corinthians while he was in Ephesus. Although this letter is called First Corinthians, verse 9 of Chapter 5 reminds the readers that Paul has written before. First Corinthians 7:1 makes clear that members of the church had written to Paul as well. Clearly, Paul and the church at Corinth were important to one another.

Letters were apparently going back and forth because the church at Corinth had a lot of problems. People were fighting with one another. Factions developed as the church members chose sides. The people were not treating one another with love and compassion. There were also questions about the way they worshiped God.

Paul gives the church members much guidance about marriage, being a Christian in a non-Christian world, worship, the Resurrection, and plans for the church. In a nutshell, Paul says that the church's problems could be resolved if people simply loved one another. First Corinthians 13 is one of the most beautiful and beloved chapters in the Bible. Paul describes love as patient, kind, supportive, trusting, loyal, and unfailing. He points out that love is not jealous, arrogant, proud, rude, selfish, or quick-tempered. Faith, hope, and love are all important; but the greatest of these is love. Paul's words to the Corinthians remind us that all who follow Christ are to love all others.

Pulling Together

Loving One Another

Remember that one of the reasons Paul is writing to the church at Corinth is that the members are having trouble getting along with one another. Factions and cliques have formed as different people choose sides and argue with one another.

Suppose you were asked to write to the youth group at Whispering Rock Church. What advice would you give them about dealing with their problems in a loving way? Here's their situation:

Some of the group members are in the habit of whispering behind people's backs. They have criticized Jasmine for being too smart (she's on the honor roll), Ben for being stuck-up (he keeps quiet because some people laugh at whatever he says), and Dionne for dressing in outdated clothes (her parents were in a serious auto accident and have not been able to return to work full-time). Several people have left the group because of the clique's actions. Some members feel that Jasmine, Ben, and Dionne will be the next to go.

Create a Loving World

The world seems to be filled with hatred and violence. People of different countries and ethnic groups are fighting. Neighbors hurl insults across the fence. Physical and emotional abuse occurs within families. Churches can be torn apart by members who insist that things be done their way.

Suppose people began to practice the kind of godly love that Paul wrote about in 1 Corinthians 13. The Greek word for this kind of generous, self-giving love is *agape* (a-GA-pay). Imagine a world filled with *agape*. What would a loving family be like? How would neighbors act? How would church members treat one another and those who visit? How would people of different nationalities or ethnic groups deal with one another? What do you suppose would be God's response to the ideal world that you and your classmates imagine?

Jesus Speaks About Love

Jesus had much to say about loving other people (including enemies!), about loving him, and about loving God. Read at least three of the selected passages below. In the space provided, write a few words or phrases to explain in your own words what you think Jesus is saying about love.

Matthew 5:43-48:

Matthew 22:37-39 (See also the sources of Jesus' quotes, Deuteronomy 6:5 and Leviticus 19:18.):

Luke 6:32-36:

Luke 7:36-50 (See especially verse 47.):

Luke 11:42:

John 12:25:

John 13:34-35:

John 14:15:

John 14:21-24:

John 14:30-31:

John 15:9-10:

John 15:12-17:

John 17:25-26:

John 21:15-17:

Paul says that love is patient and kind. Recall a recent situation in which you showed love for someone by acting with patience and kindness. Maybe your brother was annoying you, and you were nice to him rather than getting angry. Perhaps a grouchy neighbor snapped at you, and you responded with a pleasant comment. How did your loving response make you feel? What difference do you think your love made in the other person's life? (You may want to record your thoughts.)

Paul also writes that love is not jealous. Yet, you may be jealous of a friend of yours who associates with some other people you don't like. Perhaps you envy the clothes or the car of a classmate. Or possibly you get upset when someone you are dating decides to go out with other people. Are you jealous? If so, try to identify the cause of your jealousy. Spend some time in prayer asking God to help you get rid of your envy so that you can love others as God loves them.

The chorus of a familiar hymn says, "They'll know we are Christians by our love." Think carefully about your own speech, actions, and attitudes. How do you show love to others by what you say and do? What changes do you need to make with God's help so as to be more loving? (You may want to write your thoughts in the space below.)

Celebrating the Journey

Inside the heart outline, write a short definition or a poem, such as one of these three items:

➤ Write these words inside the heart and fill in your own description: Love is . . .

➤ Write a Japanese haiku, which is a short poem having three unrhymed lines of five, seven, and five syllables each. Here is an example:

Love makes me want to
sing, and shout, and dance for joy;
God's love shines through you.

➤ Write a cinquain, which is a five-line, unrhymed poem. (See the example that follows.)

Love
remembers not
the hurts of the past
but rejoices in
the hope of tomorrow.

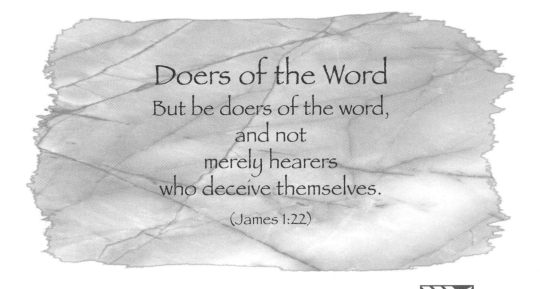

Doers of the Word
But be doers of the word,
and not
merely hearers
who deceive themselves.

(James 1:22)

Searching For...

> ➤ what true religion is all about
> ➤ the blessing that comes from acting on faith
> ➤ ways that I can put my own faith into action
> ➤ I also want to know . . .

Setting Out on the Journey

1. Read James 1:19-27.
2. Try to state in your own words at least three important points that James makes in these verses.

3. Look into a mirror for ten seconds. Then try to draw your face, or write a description of it. Look again at the mirror. How well did you do? What point is James trying to make with the mirror illustration in 1:23-24?

Getting Your Bearings

Review James 1:19-27 to see how it points you in these directions:

➤ James encourages Christians to act in ways that are pleasing to God.
➤ Being a Christian includes more than just talking about beliefs. Christians are to obey God by putting their faith into action.
➤ Christians are to be careful about what they say.
➤ True religion—the kind that pleases God—involves caring for people who need special help.

Exploring the Past

The Book of James is a letter likely written to Jewish Christians around A.D. 100. Rather than writing about particular problems in any specific church, James speaks in general about the importance of remaining faithful to God in the midst of trials and testing. He also deals with wealth, its just uses, and the tension between the rich and the poor. James offers wisdom and guidance for practical living.

Scholars have debated the identity of James. The author may have been the brother of Jesus who headed the church in Jerusalem (see Acts 15:13). More likely he was someone else who was younger but who was familiar with the teachings of Jesus. Several points made in James are similar to what Jesus said in the Sermon on the Mount.

James's emphasis on the importance of living out one's beliefs through action has caused some people, including a leader of the Protestant Reformation, Martin Luther, to question the value of this letter. The problem is that James's words have sometimes been understood to mean that Christians have to work their way into heaven. But that's not what James is saying. He wants Christians to be "doers of the word," to act, rather than just to say that they believe a certain doctrine without taking any action to show others what God's love is all about.

Pulling Together

Doing for Others

James writes about a practical religion, one in which believers do things to help people in need. In his day, widows and orphans needed special care (1:27). Men provided the family's income; so if the father died, the wife and children were left without money.

Brainstorm with your classmates to identify some groups of people in your own community who need special care. Then think about what you can do together to help these people. The list under "Doing the Word" (on page 108) may give you some ideas. Try to create a definite plan of action.

Quick to Listen, Slow to Speak, Slow to Anger

Roleplay one or more of the following situations with the other group members. Do each one twice. The first time, have one person portray a *terrible listener* who butts into the conversation. One or more persons may get angry. The second time, the players should practice good listening skills and, even if they disagree with one another, talk about their differences rather than becoming angry with one another.

➤ *Situation 1*: Lucas' mom told him not to take the car out because the roads were slick. She wasn't home, so he decided to make a quick trip to the video rental store, which was only half a mile away. Although he was driving carefully, another driver skidded into Lucas, damaging the car. He arrived home unhurt but had to face telling his mom about the accident.

➤ *Situation 2*: Caitlin no longer wanted to be an acolyte because most of the others were in elementary school. She felt she was too old for the job. When the worship chairperson called to see if Caitlin would serve the following month, Caitlin's mother said yes without first asking her daughter. The two of them are having a discussion about this matter.

➤ *Situation 3*: Hartley's brother Daniel was becoming a real problem. Although he was only in fourth grade, Daniel wanted to go with his older brother and his friends to the mall, to sports events, and other places. Hartley's parents thought that their older son, who had always been so kind to his little brother, should take Daniel places regularly. After Hartley complained about the situation, the whole family sat down to talk.

Doing the Word

Here are some ideas to help you and your group put your faith into action:

➤ Help repair a home or build a Habitat for Humanity house.

➤ Tell a friend about Jesus.

➤ Visit someone who is sick.

➤ Support a missions project or a missionary family.

➤ Serve a breakfast at the church to raise money for missions.

➤ Distribute copies of a brochure prepared by the pastor and other leaders that tells people about your church and its ministry.

➤ Collect food for a soup kitchen.

➤ Do yard work for a neighbor who is physically unable to do it.

➤ Baby-sit for several hours for free for a family in need.

➤ Ask a friend who does not usually go to church to attend Sunday school and worship with you.

➤ Set up a recycling center at the church. Provide information to show how recycling is good stewardship of the Earth.

➤ Pick up litter along a highway, or pull debris from a stream. Help others recognize that such work shows care for God's creation.

➤ Put on a Christian concert with members from your youth group. Invite the community to attend.

➤ Write a newsletter that tells what the youth in your church are doing. Have extra copies printed so that you may give them to friends and classmates who are looking for a church home.

➤ Call or write a letter to an elected official stating why your faith prompts you to support or oppose particular legislation.

➤ Volunteer to be a tutor. Do your teaching lovingly and patiently, just as Jesus did.

➤ Encourage your youth group to sponsor a family who needs assistance at Christmas or Thanksgiving. See your gift-giving as an opportunity to do God's word.

James says that everyone is to be "quick to listen, slow to speak, slow to anger" (1:19). How good are you at listening to what someone else has to say before you jump in with your own comments? Do you "fly off the handle," getting angry at the least little insult? Suppose you took James's words seriously. What habits would you need to change in your own life? (You may want to record your thoughts here.)

James writes that Christians are to be "doers of the word." That is, faith is to be put into action. Being a "doer of the word" can be difficult, however, when you don't believe that your actions will make any difference. The author Edward Everett Hale (1822–1909) states an important truth about what one person can accomplish:

> I am only one,
> But still I am one.
> I cannot do everything,
> But I can do something;
> And because I cannot do everything
> I will not refuse to do the something that I can do.

Think about these words. Is there some situation at home, at school, around the community, or at work that calls you to put your faith into action? Perhaps you thought that you couldn't make a difference, so you decided not to bother trying. Spend some time in silence listening for God to tell you what you can do, even if your action will not completely change the situation or solve the problem.

Read James 2:14-16. Can you think of a time when you said you had faith but ignored someone who needed your help? We all make mistakes like that. Remember that God forgives us. What if you could relive that episode? What would you do? How could you show by your actions that you are truly a "doer of the word"?

The Prayer of Saint Francis

(by Francis of Assisi, Italy, thirteenth century)

Lord, make me an instrument of thy peace;
where there is hatred, let me sow love;
where there is injury, pardon;
where there is doubt, faith;
where there is despair, hope;
where there is darkness, light;
and where there is sadness, joy.

O Divine Master,
grant that I may not so much seek
to be consoled as to console;
to be understood, as to understand;
to be loved, as to love;
for it is in giving that we receive,
it is in pardoning that we are pardoned,
and it is in dying that we are born to eternal life. [1]

In what ways is God calling you to be a doer of the word?

---

[1] Taken from *The United Methodist Hymnal*, 481.

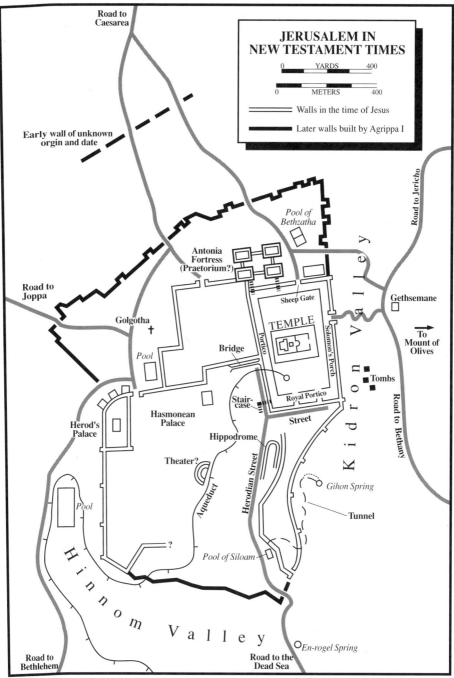

JERUSALEM IN NEW TESTAMENT TIMES

0   YARDS   400

0   METERS   400

Walls in the time of Jesus

Later walls built by Agrippa I

Road to Caesarea

Early wall of unknown orgin and date

Road to Jericho

Pool of Bethzatha

Antonia Fortress (Praetorium?)

Road to Joppa

Sheep Gate

Gethsemane

Golgotha

TEMPLE

To Mount of Olives

Portico

Pool

Bridge

Solomon's Porch

Tombs

Staircase

Royal Portico

Street

Hasmonean Palace

Herod's Palace

Hippodrome

Theater?

Herodian Street

Kidron Valley

Road to Bethany

Aqueduct

Gihon Spring

Pool

Tunnel

?

Pool of Siloam

Hinnom Valley

En-rogel Spring

Road to Bethlehem

Road to the Dead Sea

© United Bible Societies, 1976

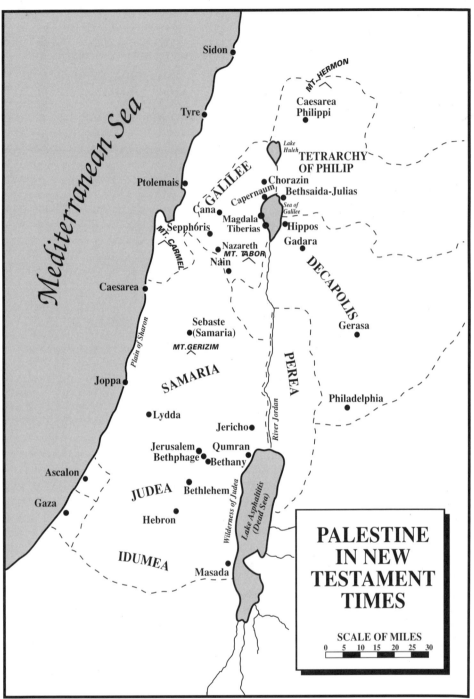

Sidon

MT. HERMON

Caesarea
Philippi

Lake
Huleh

TETRARCHY
OF PHILIP

Tyre

Mediterranean Sea

Ptolemais

GALILEE

Chorazin

Capernaum

Bethsaida-Julias

Cana

Sea of
Galilee

Sepphoris

Magdala
Tiberias

Hippos

MT. CARMEL

Nazareth
MT. TABOR

Gadara

Nain

DECAPOLIS

Caesarea

Plain of Sharon

Sebaste
(Samaria)

MT. GERIZIM

Gerasa

SAMARIA

PEREA

Joppa

Philadelphia

Lydda

Jericho

River Jordan

Jerusalem
Bethphage

Qumran

Bethany

Ascalon

JUDEA

Bethlehem

Wilderness of Judea

Lake Asphaltitis
(Dead Sea)

Gaza

Hebron

PALESTINE
IN NEW
TESTAMENT
TIMES

IDUMEA

Masada

SCALE OF MILES

0   5   10   15   20   25   30

ESSENTIAL BIBLE PASSAGES FOR YOUTH